TREASURE
ISLANDS

TREASURE ISLANDS

THE WOMAN'S HOUR GUIDE TO CHILDREN'S READING
JULIA ECCLESHARE

BBC BOOKS

For Henry, Edward and Vanessa

Published by BBC Books,
a division of BBC Enterprises Limited,
Woodlands, 80 Wood Lane, London W12 0TT

First published 1988 © Julia Eccleshare 1988

ISBN 0 563 20691 8 (paperback)
ISBN 0 563 20727 2 (hardback)

Set in 10½ on 13pt Goudy by Ace Filmsetting Ltd, Frome, Somerset
Printed and bound in Great Britain by Redwood Burn Ltd, Trowbridge, Wiltshire
Cover printed by Fletchers of Norwich

Contents

Our thanks are due to the following publishers for their kind permission to reproduce copyright illustrations:
Faber and Faber Ltd: *The Iron Man* by Ted Hughes, illustrated by Andrew Davidson, 1985 (p.9); William Collins Sons & Co Ltd: *Tom Fobble's Day* by Alan Garner, illustrated by Michael Foreman, 1979 (p.11); The Bodley Head: *Katie Morag Delivers the Mail* by Mairi Hedderwick, 1984 (p.19); Andersen Press Ltd: *Going West* by Martin Waddell, illustrated by Philippe Dupasquier, 1983 (pp.20,21); The Bodley Head: *Rosie's Walk* by Pat Hutchins, 1968 (p.24); Walker Books Ltd: *Me and My Friend* by Alan Ahlberg, illustrated by Colin McNaughton, 1986 (pp.27,111); Jonathan Cape Ltd: *John Patrick Norman McHennessy – the boy who was always late* by John Burningham, 1987 (p.52); Methuen & Co Ltd: *Flat Stanley* by Jeff Brown, illustrated by Toni Ungerer, 1964 (p.59); Victor Gollancz Ltd: *The Sheep-Pig* by Dick King-Smith, illustrated by Mary Rayner, 1983 (p.61); Methuen & Co Ltd: *Little House in the Big Woods* by Laura Ingalls Wilder, illustrated by Garth Williams (p.69); Victor Gollancz Ltd: *Carrie's War* by Nina Bawden, illustrated by Faith Jaques, 1973 (p.71); Century Hutchinson Publishing Group Ltd: *The Woman in the Moon* by James Riordan, (p.80); André Deutsch Ltd: *Axe-Age, Wolf-Age* by Kevin Crossley-Holland, illustrated by Hannah Firmin, 1985 (p.84); Puffin Books: *Handles* by Jan Mark, illustrated by David Parkins, 1983 (p.91); Julia MacRae Books: *Piggybook* by Anthony Browne, 1986 (p.96); André Deutsch Ltd: *Quick, Let's Get Out of Here!* by Michael Rosen, illustrated by Quentin Blake, 1983 (p.107).

Our thanks are also due to the following who have given us permission to reprint poems from their collections:
Faber and Faber Ltd: 'Poetry' by 'Peter' from *Messages: A Book of Poems* compiled by Naomi Lewis (p.103); Faber and Faber Ltd: 'The Night Mail' by W. H. Auden, from *Collected Poems* (p.106); Gareth Owen: 'Street Cricket' by Gareth Owen from *Salford Road* (p.107); André Deutsch Ltd: 'Eddie and the Nappy' by Michael Rosen, from *Quick, Let's Get Out of Here!* (p.107); Peters Fraser & Dunlop Group Ltd: 'Zebra Crossing' by Roger McGough, from *Sky in the Pie* (p.108); the Estate of Robert Frost: 'Stopping by Woods on a Snowy Evening' by Robert Frost, from *The Poetry of Robert Frost*, ed. Edward Connery Lathem (pub. Jonathan Cape Ltd), (p.108); Penguin Books Ltd: 'Squeezes' by Brian Patten, from *Gargling with Jelly* (p.108).

Foreword

PENELOPE LIVELY

CHILDREN'S BOOKS are far too much fun – and far too interesting – to be left to children. *Treasure Islands* – the brainchild of its producer, Sally Feldman, who does all the hard work behind the scenes – invites parents, teachers, librarians, indeed anyone, to share the pleasures and the issues raised. Discussion of new books is one element, meeting authors and illustrators is another. But the matter of what children are to read sends ripples in all directions – it raises questions about how children are best taught to read in the first place, whether or not children's books should be a vehicle for social engineering (do we need special books for ethnic minorities?), and it has implications for the publishing industry and how that operates.

People have always been aware of the potential power of children's literature. Give a child a book, and you are embarking on the vital and insidious process of shaping his or her view of the world. Once upon a time there were fairy stories. There still are. But they were never as simple as they might appear; they made moral recommendations, they reflected people's fears, they made psychological revelations. It has been ever thus. What is written for children, the way in which it is written, fashions and foibles in children's literature, are all manifestations of thought and behaviour in a particular time and society – and not just thoughts connected with children. The Victorians saw children's books as social and moral tracts – written to inspire a proper terror of death and damnation and to shore up the class structure. Victorian didacticism is far from defunct; plenty of people still see children's books as primarily instructive – not just in the sense of teaching facts but also teaching attitudes, inculcating proper views about race or sex or society. Should books reflect the world, or should they manipulate it? This is a central problem in all literature, of course – and in children's books it takes on a special edge.

The English tradition of children's literature has always been maverick and unique. It has produced the great classics. *Alice in Wonderland* broke the mould of Victorian piety and paved the way for Edith Nesbit, for *The Wind in the Willows*, for Beatrix Potter and A. A. Milne and the children's novel of today. We are fortunate. The English literary tradition has found a special place for children's books and we are the richer for it. In return for taking them seriously we have reaped a superb harvest of fun, eccentricity and revelation. They are central to the language and to the culture. People who may never have read Lewis Carroll talk about 'a grin like a Cheshire cat's'; the language has an independent life, like the language of Shakespeare or the Bible.

It is independent, though, only up to a point. The books – the best of them – transcend time and place but they still depend on us, on our continued response to them. Most children do not come upon books unaided. They rely upon teachers, librarians, and above all parents. I once acquired a car sticker which I flaunted proudly until the car to which it was stuck wore out. It said, simply, 'WHEN DID YOU LAST READ TO A CHILD?' Quite so. The last thirty years have seen an alliance between the producers of children's books – writers, illustrators, publishers – and the educational world which has done an enormous amount to bring good books to more children than ever before. Teachers and librarians have recognised that it is not enough to teach children to read, but that you must then give them something worth reading. At its best, this is a fruitful and creative connection. It's certainly an essential one. But books should not be associated just with the classroom – they should be everywhere: in the home, in the pocket, under the bedclothes. The sharing of books with children is a vital aspect of being a parent – as well as one of the most agreeable. My own children have long since grown up, but that sensation of a small bony behind grinding into your lap as you read aloud from some battered old favourite is one of my most cherished memories.

The range of children's books today is immense. What is there for babies? For a seven-year-old hooked on dinosaurs? How can we seduce a book-rejecting adolescent? Julia Eccleshare offers an excellent guide through the maze of titles available, along with a valuable discussion of some of the crucial issues in children's literature today.

Introduction

SIFTING AND SELECTING the books discussed here has been a most enjoyable job. It has meant thinking carefully about what makes a good book of any kind, why some books last and others don't, and how far children's and adults' tastes in books differ from one another. It has meant working out what is special about all the books that I like and the ones that my children like. One of the nicest things has been re-reading not my own favourites, which I already know backwards, but all the other books which other people have raised and which I have also come to love.

But it has been a hard task too. There is no problem about what to put *in*. The difficulty comes in deciding what to leave *out*. Throughout, I have chosen books that I like, while also aiming to cover the main areas of fiction and the most successful books in those areas. I have tried to choose the important titles, rather than anything particularly idiosyncratic, so that each book will make its point boldly and clearly to as wide an audience as possible.

While I believe that all these books are well written they are not all of equal literary excellence. Some have been chosen for their exact suitability for a particular audience rather than for fine stylistic qualities. The books listed as 'Further reading' at the end of each chapter are every bit as significant as those in the main text. Anyone who reads the books mentioned in any part of this book will have a sure base from which to read on and on. Fitting particular books into particular categories has also been difficult. Most books can be described in many different ways, so I hope that no one is going to ignore a book just because here it must be restricted to being of a particular type.

When choosing books for children it is important to know the difference between good and bad. It is important to choose carefully but it is also vital to remember that reading is fun. Remembering that will lead to the best choices of all.

READING ALOUD

CHAPTER ONE

TO BEGIN AT the beginning, as all the best story books do, I shall start with reading aloud – one of the easiest activities for a parent and one of the cosiest for a child. Sitting with a child on your knee and looking at the pictures in a book or reading a story is far more restful than doing puzzles or making playdough shapes. It also has very particular long-term effects. 5

Babies need both reassurance and stimulation. They need a secure base and they also need to develop an interest in the world around them and their skills in understanding and appreciating it – hearing, seeing, touching, smelling and tasting. Parents need props to make all this possible and books are the best way of fulfilling most of these needs, hearing and seeing most obviously. Using the words of a rhyme or story with a child who cannot talk provides a link between parent and child when conversation can only be one-way. A verse of a nursery rhyme or the words of a story do not need an answer. They can be comforting, exciting or even a little frightening, according to mood or need.

All parents need a good selection of rhymes, finger games, and lullabies, such as the ones in *Mother Goose Treasury* by Raymond Briggs or Sarah Pooley's *A Day of Rhymes*. The words of a rhyme such as 'It's raining, it's pouring, The old man is snoring' are considerably more descriptive than a straight statement of fact, while the simple 'Hush-a-bye baby on the tree top' has a timeless calm. These soothing, rocking, teasing, explanatory rhymes have a very special place in children's earliest memories. And as a parent it is surprising how many nursery rhymes one can remember, even if only in fragments. These collections of rhymes and their accompanying illustrations lead naturally to the treasure house of picture books with simple texts described in the next chapter. Babies can respond to these books and be entertained by them, long before they can speak.

Reading aloud to a child who *can* talk is a very different activity but, so long as that child cannot read, there is no doubt that it serves a valuable purpose. Now the listening child is able to interact. Children's delight is always completely obvious and they will make it equally apparent when they are bored stiff by what you are reading to them. While these children still love sharing picture books they are also able to enjoy longer stories and this is a time when collections such as Judith Elkin's *The New Golden Land Anthology* or Sara and Stephen Corrin's *Stories for Five-Year-Olds* and *Stories for Six-Year-Olds*, or Virginia Haviland and Raymond Briggs's *The Fairy Tale Treasury* are invaluable. Fairy stories, folk stories, myths and legends are some of the very best stories for reading aloud. They have been retold in many forms, as described in Chapter Eight. Though started in picture book form and read from an early age, these stories will continue to entertain all age groups.

Some of the most enjoyable stories to read aloud come from Rudyard Kipling's half-fantastical, half-realistic tales about animals, the *Just So Stories*. They are wordy and full of difficult vocabulary, which means that they are lost to all but the very best readers unless they are read aloud. No one who has heard 'How the Rhinoceros Got His Skin' will be able to escape from the horrible tickling and scratching sensation of those crumbs buttoned in under the skin. And all curious children will identify with the poor old elephant's child whose relatives spank him 'immediately and directly, without stopping, for a long time', all on account of his 'satiable curtiosity'. (Parents of such children may well feel very like the intolerant relatives!)

Collections of any kind, whether folk and fairy tales or contemporary ones, have the advantage of offering a broad spectrum of stories to suit the mood of the listener, as well as appealing to a wide age range, which is important if you are reading to more than one child. Picture books and stories in collections also lend themselves to being read over and over again. For both reader and listener this seems quite fitting, while reading a whole book aloud time and again can seem like marking time. Knowing a story off by heart means that the children know what is going to happen next. But they like this. Far from spoiling any surprise element, it enhances their sense of enjoyment, just as knowing a piece of music makes it easier for the listener to understand and appreciate it.

The brevity of the stories in a collection makes them especially suitable for reading aloud in a single evening. Very young children need a complete story a night but, as their concentration and their memories improve, they start to enjoy longer 'chapter' books which have quite different qualities. There is much security in knowing something about the book and there is the anticipation of what you don't know and what might happen next. Through books of this kind the ideas of continuity and construction of a plot are established.

The eye-stretching exploits of Dorothy Edwards's heroine in *My Naughty Little Sister* have held three-year-olds and upwards spellbound with delight for over twenty years. Though now rather old-fashioned in feel, these stories capture the home life and close interaction between mother, child and younger sister in a sympathetic and humorous way. Anne Strugnall's more contemporary *The Julian Stories* revolve around a small boy, his brother and their domestic activities which will be reassuringly familiar to young listeners. Stories like these, which centre on the home and the family, provide a comforting contrast to the more violent and challenging world of many fairy stories.

There are other stories in the same gentle vein which also offer security but combine it with an imaginary element. Rumer Godden's stories of two Japanese dolls who have a real life of their own, such as *Miss Happiness and Miss Flower*, appeal to children who have the imagination to see that their own dolls could also be like this. T. R. Bear similarly comes to life in *T. R. Bear Goes to School* (by Terrance Dicks) and causes all sorts of problems and successes for his owner. This is an altogether more humorous and rumbustious world than Rumer Godden's but the imaginative quality is very much the same.

All these different kinds of stories offer entertainment and enrichment long before children can possibly read for themselves. Hearing someone read stories aloud is instrumental in preparing the ground for learning to read. Through sharing and finding pleasure in books from the very beginning children get the idea that books are an enjoyable part of life. More specifically, and with a very direct bearing on learning to read, they find out what reading is *for*, which makes them much more likely to want to do it.

7

No one questions the good sense of reading aloud before a child can read. At its most basic it is the only way the child can find out what is in that book. But then there is a long period when children can read simple texts such as *The Big Honey Hunt* (described in Chapter Three) but when their comprehension of story far outstrips their own reading skills. At this point, when reading aloud may begin to seem redundant – or even a substitute for children reading to themselves – it still provides the opportunity to enjoy far more difficult books than they could manage on their own and, more importantly, it plays a vital role in encouraging the beginner to struggle with simple texts. Children hearing a story read aloud can comprehend difficult words and concepts. They need this way of moving on in reading but not at the expense of being offered everything too young. There is no prescribed order in which books should be read or heard but it is a shame to miss out on the books suitable for a particular age group. Their appeal may be diminished later on.

Choose books which excite and stimulate but consider your audience carefully. There is nothing superior about a young child 'knowing' a difficult book like *The Hobbit* by J. R. R. Tolkien (though that is an easy trap for parents to fall into). Books for the right age group will offer specific things which are appropriate for them emotionally. On the other hand, a listener who is too young will miss many of the finer points and much of the subtlety of a book which they may understand superficially but not fully comprehend.

Your own child's taste will affect what you – or they – choose for reading aloud. Almost any book can be read aloud (even encyclopedias), though 'story' is usually the absolute key. The audience response will soon tell you whether a book is working or not. Some books are especially suited to being read aloud, and some are written especially for it. As a poet, Ted Hughes well knows the importance of reading aloud. He called *The Iron Man* 'A Children's Story in Five Nights', and its simple structure, brevity and taut drama make it perfect for reading aloud. Ted Hughes wastes no words in the five short chapters of the book, which starts with the Iron Man's spectacular C-R-A-S-H over the edge of the cliff and ends as a tense fight between good and evil high in the sky.

Not all books have such a specific intention but a strong drama neatly contained in a series of chapters lends itself to 'a chapter a night'

8

9

THE IRON MAN

treatment. Jill Murphy's stories of Miss Cackle's Academy and poor, unsuccessful Mildred in *The Worst Witch* make excellent and amusing listening. There is a build-up of drama but each chapter also has a strong incident of its own. *Clever Polly and the Stupid Wolf* by Catherine Storr is written with each chapter as a separate story but within each chapter children will be anxious to know how Polly will outwit the wolf next. There is reassurance and a lot of fun here too, and Polly always does escape from the wolf – in the end.

Even when children have become fluent and well-established readers their comprehension of stories that are read aloud will still outstrip what they can understand when reading to themselves. At this stage, starting off a story aloud to get a child launched into a book which they might not be prepared to tackle alone can influence the choice of what to read aloud next. *Moonfleet* by J. Meade Falkner is a vividly dramatic smuggling adventure, but the style is old-fashioned and could be offputting. Writers of the nineteenth and early twentieth century are wordier than contemporary authors but the stories they tell deserve as wide an audience as possible. Among contemporary writers, too, there are those whose complexity can seem daunting before the story is fully under way. Alan Garner's *Tom Fobble's Day* is a superbly written book but it is not an easy one for a child to read. Alan Garner has consistently pushed against conventional novelistic forms, both in overall shape and sentence structure. A confident and experienced reader can cope but there are lots of readers who might be deterred and would therefore miss an outstanding and original story which would be perfectly comprehensible if read aloud.

10

But reading aloud is more than just a way of easing the reader into a book. As a natural extension of the storytelling tradition that has evolved from the sagas and ballads passed down from one generation to another, it has a special quality even in a time of newer and more sophisticated media. It lacks the flexibility and individuality of storytelling but it preserves the special, interactive experience of the reader, the book and the listener. The reader and listener are hearing the same story at the same time and they are sharing their enjoyment with each other. It is a collective experience in which responses – laughter, sorrow or tension – are often far more intense than when the story is read alone. This means that a story shared can seem very different to a story read alone. Since pre-reading children are the accepted audience for reading aloud, some children pretend that they cannot read just so that they will not be denied the delight of having books read to them.

Babies have the privilege of being read to at any time of day – or even night. As children get older, reading aloud is usually confined to bedtime in the hope that it will be a soothing way of helping them get to sleep. This is sheer practicality. Obviously, there is no reason why books cannot be read aloud at any time. In some families reading aloud takes place at meals because it is a time when there is a captive audience.

The difficulty of competing with other media is a real one. Before television became such a universal presence, evenings at home might

11

well have included some reading aloud. Certainly it would have been the obvious form of entertainment for a family with the time for reading and the money for books, especially for those who delighted in any kind of fantasy or in entering worlds beyond their own. Today, many families have too little time or energy to devote to reading aloud. This is an enormous loss in terms of entertainment but, more than that, it works against the later development of children's reading. In view of the wealth of literature which could be available as they grow older, reading aloud is an activity which should not be squeezed out – whatever the cost.

12

FURTHER READING

JAMES REEVES *The Gnome Factory and Other Stories*, illustrated by Edward Ardizzone, Puffin

This is a wonderful collection of stories of all kinds. Some are James Reeves's own, others are his fresh retellings of traditional folk and fairy tales such as 'Rapunzel' and 'The Secret Shoemakers'. There is a lot of magic in these stories as well as humour and fantasy. All of them, whatever their origins, are lively and vivid.   (7+)

JOAN AIKEN *A Necklace of Raindrops*, illustrated by Jan Pieńkowski, Puffin

Joan Aiken has a particular ability to blend magic and reality so well that it is impossible to spot the seams. In this collection of eight stories she brings her special touch to such ordinary things as a pile of books and a baker's cat. Her belief in magic is absolute and infectious.

(6+)

LEON GARFIELD *Shakespeare Stories*, illustrated by Michael Foreman, Gollancz

Purists will feel that Shakespeare is Shakespeare and that he should not be tampered with, but *Shakespeare Stories* may convince them otherwise. Leon Garfield uses his own skills as a storyteller in the chilling story of 'Macbeth', the lyrical romance of 'Romeo and Juliet', the tragedy of 'Othello' and many others. His prose echoes the poetic originals while being entirely comprehensible to a much younger audience. Both the atmosphere and the meaning of these marvellous stories remain intact.   (9+)

TERRY JONES *Nicobobinus*, illustrated by Michael Foreman, Puffin

This is an original and fanciful adventure story. Nicobobinus and his friend Rosie set out from their home in Venice to discover the Land of Dragons. From the unusual departure onwards there is helter-skelter action, with danger, surprises, successes, failures and excitement crowding on each other. Terry Jones has written a won-derful fairy story which is an entirely successful combination of magic, mystery, adventure and humour.   (7+)

13

JULIUS LESTER (RETELLER) *The Tales of Uncle Remus: The Adventures of Brer Rabbit*, illustrated by Jerry Pinkney, Bodley Head

Brer Fox, Brer Rabbit, Brer Lion, Brer Tiger, Brer Dog and Brer Wolf – the Uncle Remus stories revolve around all the animals, their interaction with each other and with Mr Man. Cunning and trickery are the animals' main skills, though speed and agility sometimes play a part too. The Uncle Remus stories are witty and sharp. Julius Lester's retold version captures their Afro-American origins while making the stories accessible to a contemporary audience.   (6+)

14

PICTURE BOOKS

CHAPTER TWO

BABIES, EVEN THE tiniest ones, can enjoy books. Sharing a book with a baby is a natural extension of just holding it in your arms or on your knee. It requires no special skill and no equipment beyond the book itself. Babies need rhymes and words and verbal patterns, all of which come from the first jiggling, joggling nursery rhymes. And, very soon, they can do more than just listen. They can look around them and be stimulated by many and varied images. They need colours and shapes and patterns and explanations of what such things are. They are also ready to put the looking and listening together.

With looking and listening go touching, smelling and even tasting. Babies 'pick' ice-creams off pages and lick them, they 'smell' the flowers that are shown in the pictures, they 'kiss' the dolls and the teddies. It's part of their way of enjoying a book. The children who love books are the ones who know everything about them, the ones who turn the pages backwards and forwards on their own, even at the risk of a tear or crease. Books are precious but they are not priceless or, usually, irreplaceable. Their preciousness is what is *inside*. They cannot be enjoyed by children if they are surrounded by 'Private – Keep Out' or 'Do Not Touch' notices.

The first impression of anything new needs to be a good one. Giving babies the best from the very beginning will be the surest way of making them see books as a source of real pleasure. The mass of picture books makes this easy to do. Board books have particular advantages at the chewing and tearing stage, because their laminated covers make them child-proof, although their content usually has a considerably shorter life. These board books are specifically aimed at the very young, with most sticking to a simple image on each page and either no text or the briefest of labelling texts. Their success lies in the appropriateness of the concept behind the book and the very high quality of the illustration.

Helen Oxenbury has produced the most delicious board books which, with her delicate artwork and easy humour, capture the minutiae of baby life. They are reassuring in both their setting and tone. *Helping* shows the baby doing its best with washing-up and hoovering. There is a lot of enthusiasm but a lot of mess too, just as there is in real life. *Family* includes Mum, Dad, grandparents, brothers and sisters in a close relationship with the baby. The baby listening and looking sees itself cuddling in Dad's jacket or being held rather too eagerly by an older sibling. Their popularity shows that a discriminating eye for good-quality artwork and subtle humour can be developed right from the beginning.

High-quality photography has also been widely used in board books. Camilla Jessell's *Baby's Days* and *Baby's Toys* have a domestic setting. Fiona Pragoff, similarly, concentrates on things that are familiar to the baby consumer. Her *Alphabet* makes use of objects that commonly surround a baby – a popular make of toy garage found in many households, a baby's shoes and socks – while *Growing* gives the toddler some instructive, entertaining and brightly coloured photographs of a growing baby. With or without text, these books make good looking, pointing and *talking* material. They are books that can be fingered, licked, sucked, carried in prams, dropped and taken to bed. They show babies the fun and value of books and they don't need to be revered.

But board books are not a substitute for picture books. There are picture books in traditional formats which involve babies by inviting interaction, even at the risk of torn flaps or enlarged holes. Eric Carle's *The Very Hungry Caterpillar*, which shows how the tiny caterpillar eats its way – literally – through one green leaf, two apples, three pears and so on, until it is huge and fat and turns into a beautiful butterfly, is especially successful. The clever use of holes and half-page flaps encourages children to touch and get to know the book. *Where's Spot?* and its sequels by Eric Hill have the same interactive quality. Lifting the flaps in the search for Spot reveals pictures and words which are central to the main text. Books like these engage the listener by gaining their active co-operation. Once the pattern of parent and child sitting together sharing a book, or a child on their own leafing through a book (or a parent doing the same!) has been established, the only other problem is a luxury. Which book to choose?

Picture books today are of an exceptionally high standard. Illustrators and artists are putting their talents into creating good-quality, suitable artwork for children. They are entertaining children as well as training them to look closely, and to respond to the subtleties of drawing and painting. Just as hearing is vital in developing language, so looking carefully is important to children's visual development and their emerging tastes.

But a picture book consists of more than just pretty, striking or funny pictures. It must also have a text which suits the illustrations. The words must fit well with the artwork and they must make a good story in themselves. Too many picture books are spoilt by texts which are poor stories. Others are good stories but not ones that particularly lend themselves to being matched with illustrations. Both text and pictures must offer involvement and subtlety – two important elements in entertainment. Books should make children feel amused, surprised, frightened or comforted. Looking closely at the artwork should reward them with the discovery of an unexpected treasure which may become the thing they most remember about that particular book. Children who are used to looking carefully often find a particular reason for liking – or *loving* – a book, which has little or nothing to do with the central storyline. It is usually a tiny detail – the way the dog is drinking from its bowl, the fact that the baby has dropped its bottle – incidentals which are crucial to the overall effect. It is these details, this commitment to understanding that children need subtleties, that give certain books their particular entertainment value. 'Reading' pictures in this way is a child's first step towards reading words.

Most of Janet and Allan Ahlberg's books break new ground in one way or another but for very young children their greatest success comes with *The Baby's Catalogue*. Here, recognising how toddlers love to pore over pictures of themselves in catalogues advertising baby products, they have produced a picture book along the same lines. Babies sleeping, getting dressed, eating breakfast, playing with their brothers and sisters, Mums, Dads, even accidents such as dropping keys down a drain, each accurate down to the minutest detail, figure in

17

this wholly child-centred book. The Ahlbergs know exactly how to involve their baby audience.

Anthony Browne's surrealist pictures may look over-sophisticated. They certainly lack the cuddly quality which is so often associated with children's illustration. But, in his own way, he knows exactly how to draw the child reader in. *Bear Hunt* has the simplest text but the artwork contains highly sophisticated jokes – flowers wearing ties, Belisha beacons with policemen's helmets on. The illustrations entice children to look closely and they are amply rewarded for doing so.

Picture books can offer reassuring images of a safe domestic world. For instance, Sarah Garland's *Going Shopping*, which shows a cheerfully harassed Mum loaded down with a baby, buggy and a dog struggling through a large supermarket, confirms a familiar experience in the life of most babies. But these books are also an excellent way of extending the child's experience. Sitting with your arm around a child provides a safe setting from which they can explore a larger and more complex world by looking at books dealing with unfamiliar experiences or approaching situations from a fresh point of view. This exploration also means learning to understand the concept of fantasy. Pushed to its limits it can also be associated with being frightened and picture books play an important role in airing and allaying fears.

Children's own experience is usually fairly restricted geographically. Urban children know parks and swings and buses and they like picture books that show these familiar places. *Alfie's Feet* by Shirley Hughes has some wonderful illustrations of a walk in the park which has been reached from a terraced house. These settings are reassuring to urban children but they also need to know what other places look like. Mairi Hedderwick gives town children an understanding of the quieter way of life on a remote Scottish island in her stories, *Katie Morag Delivers the Mail* and *Katie Morag and the Two Grandmothers*.

For country children the same applies in reverse. They need books like Errol Lloyd's *Nini at the Carnival*, which gives them a glimpse of the atmosphere – first jolly, then frightening and finally reassuring – of an event in a big city. On a larger scale, picture books provide the perfect introduction to an awareness of other countries and how different they are. *Bringing the Rain to Kapiti Plain*, by Verna Aardema, shows the parched earth and the thirsting animals far more vividly than any words.

18

Extending experiences far beyond the differences between town and country, or one country and another, are the picture books which explore different kinds of fantasy. Fantasy can mean a variety of things. It may be something wholly in the mind, as portrayed so clearly and wittily in *Time to get out of the bath, Shirley*, in which Shirley is off on a series of adventures while her Mum prattles on about washing properly, tidying the bathroom and other mundane matters. By juxtaposing Mum in the bathroom on one side of the page and Shirley slipping swiftly through the plug hole and away on her charger on the other, John Burningham makes it possible to enjoy the fantasy from the outside while also experiencing it with Shirley. Then again, the fantasy may be more along the lines of an imaginary story which *might* happen to the child listening, as in Elfrida Vipont and Raymond Briggs's *The Elephant and the Bad Baby*, where the elephant and the bad baby set off 'rumpeta, rumpeta, rumpeta all down the road' on a series of daylight robberies before going safely back home for tea with the bad baby's welcoming mummy. Either way, these stories show children what fantasy is. They offer them something beyond the everyday world. And they encourage them to develop fantasies of their own.

19

KATIE MORAG DELIVERS THE MAIL

The pictures and stories in a book, particularly those stories where the experience is clearly imaginary, are an excellent way of exploring all sorts of emotions and situations which are too frightening to tackle head-on. Children *like* – and need – to be just a little bit frightened, as long as the fear is controlled. *Where the Wild Things Are* by Maurice Sendak looks, at first glance, like a most unlikely bedtime story. In fact it has become a classic because young children identify with Max who is sent to bed without any supper, and they enjoy his romp with the Wild Things (a group of fearsome, scary monsters), safe in the knowledge that Max himself is safe and that he returns happily to his bed where a little snack has been left out for him. Knowing that Max is safe and that they themselves are far removed from such dangers makes *Where the Wild Things Are* a deliciously scary experience.

A different kind of fear is explored in the ebullient *The Trouble with Mum* by Babette Cole. 'The trouble with Mum is the hats she wears . . .' and all the other unusual things she does because she is a witch. Not a nasty witch, a nice, friendly witch; but nonetheless a bit of an embarrassment at school events, though an absolute wow with friends at home. The joke is a potentially frightening one. It raises the idea that behind an apparently normal exterior there may lie a secret and different self.

Susan Varley and Jean Willis's *Monster Bed* makes a wonderful joke out of the fears children have about going to bed. The baby monster is frightened of a human hiding under the bed. The baby human is frightened of a monster hiding under the bed. They meet and the fear is conquered. The building up and resolution of fear give children a chance to look at that fear and see it for what it *really* is. They are frightened but excited at the same time.

The particular appeal of picture books extends far beyond the very youngest children. Never let yourself or your child dismiss picture books as 'baby books'. Long past the time when children can squash on to a knee they still love the picture book format and the double 'reading' of words and pictures together.

For a child who is still not sure of words alone, the simple text of a picture book, matched by good and meaningful illustrations, provides exactly the right impetus for reading. The way in which these books work is described in Chapter Three. Later, when children are fluent readers, they still enjoy the interaction between text and pictures. The way the pictures tell the story reinforces and sometimes enlarges the words, giving the book a completely new dimension. Martin Waddell and Philippe Dupasquier's *Going West* has a brief text but the experience of a pioneering family moving out to the West of the United States in a covered wagon is fleshed out by the artwork. And the very simplicity of the text is an ideal foil to the lively artwork which shows the detail of such a journey.

The problems of a second marriage are not traditional picture book material but *The Visitors Who Came to Stay*, by Annalena McAfee and Anthony Browne, uses text and pictures to tell a story which makes its points cogently and with more subtlety than would have been possible with words alone.

The scope of picture books is limitless. They are the starting-point for the very youngest readers but their conjunction of pictures and text also lays important foundations for a child's developing powers of observation and concentration which will be so important for their later enjoyment of books.

FURTHER READING

MICHAEL FOREMAN *Dinosaurs and All That Rubbish*, Puffin

This is a deeply moral tale in picture book form. Its moral – that the Earth belongs to everyone and must be shared – is one that children should learn as soon as possible. Man's greed threatens to destroy the Earth but the long-buried dinosaurs are woken from their sleep by the changes in the ground, and return in time to clear up Man's rubbish and turn the world back into its former paradise. All that remains is to educate Man about his future role in a world that belongs to *everyone*. (4+)

SHIRLEY HUGHES *Dogger*, Fontana

Shirley Hughes's books are always full of insight into the things that are really important for small children. The Dogger of the title is Dave's much-loved toy dog which gets lost and then sold – by mistake – at a summer fête. Child listeners, the majority of whom have a favourite toy like Dogger, will empathise with Dave's utter despair when Dogger is lost. The bustling fair where everyone else is enjoying themselves provides a good contrast to Dave's wretchedness. In contrast, too, is his delight, relief and euphoria when his sister buys Dogger back. There is total happiness for Dave and his readers when the last page shows him tucked up in bed – with Dogger. (3+)

DAVID MCKEE *Not Now, Bernard*, Sparrow Books

This is a scary book, but a funny one too. Bernard finds a monster in the garden and runs in to tell his parents. Like all parents they do not listen closely to everything that Bernard says. 'Not now, Bernard' they reply. But there *is* a monster and he proceeds to eat Bernard up and then move into the house, where Mum and Dad ignore him just as they did Bernard – and with similarly disastrous results. Some children will never like this book but for many it makes just the right joke about parental detachment. (4+)

JILL MURPHY *Peace at Last*, Macmillan

Peace at Last is a book which has almost equal appeal for parents and children. While parents sympathise with Father Bear as he moves from place to place – the sitting room, the kitchen and even the garage – to get some sleep, children delight in the things, and especially the noises, that keep him awake. ' "SNORE" went Mrs Bear, "SNORE, SNORE, SNORE", "DRIP . . . DRIP" . . . went the leaky kitchen tap.' The rhythmic, repetitive text and the beautiful illustrations are equally funny. (2+)

HELEN NICHOLL and JAN PIEŃKOWSKI *Meg and Mog*, Puffin

The now long-standing success of *Meg and Mog* and all the subsequent Meg and Mog books is an excellent example of how much children love absolute simplicity and clarity in illustration. Jan Pieńkowski draws the witch Meg, her black-and-white stripey cat Mog and their friend Owl as simple outline figures which are immediately recognisable from a very early age. The texts have a simplicity too. Each one revolves around Meg's spells which have a habit of going badly wrong. Here she mistakenly turns some of her witch friends into mice. Bold and bright, unpredictable but ultimately safe with a very friendly image, these are a huge success. (1+)

23

MARY RAYNER *Mr and Mrs Pig's Evening Out*, Macmillan

Like all parents, Mr and Mrs Pig sometimes want to go out in the evening. With ten little piglets to be left at home there is a bit of difficulty finding a babysitter whom all the children will like. Mrs Pig is delighted when the agency comes up with someone suitable but she fails to notice one thing. The babysitter's name is Mrs Wolf and she has dark hairy knees . . . There follows a drama of piggy courage and sibling solidarity which makes this potentially scary book into a reassuring one. It is, however, a book that should be used with caution for children who are *really* off the idea of a babysitter. (3+)

24

ROSIE'S WALK

BECOMING
A READER

CHAPTER THREE

HERE IS NO one way of learning to read but there are a great many books which will help children get started while also showing them the ultimate point of being able to read. There are also some basic ground rules for parents. 25 The end result of learning to read is to be a real reader. Appreciating the point of a book is as important as understanding the words, since it is ultimately the relationship between the reader and the book that counts. That is why it is important to read real books from the beginning, as they will provide that relationship even if they do not speed up the learning process.

The same words are found in all books, whether they are 'readers' or not, so there is no need to choose a special kind of book for learning to read. With their restricted vocabulary and formula stories, 'readers' are often the most unlikely way of encouraging a child to read. A child who has enjoyed picture books from an early age will be depressed by the drabness of these stories and will see little point in bothering with them. If you choose any straightforward book with a simple text, the vocabulary need not be too difficult. *Rosie's Walk* by Pat Hutchins has a bold text with only one line on each page. 'Rosie the hen went for a walk' and there she is in the picture, going for a walk. The right-hand picture tells exactly the same story as the words. The left-hand picture shows what is happening to the fox meanwhile. Between the two they offer a full and funny story but written in a way that is easy to read.

The way the pictures tell the same story as the words is of enormous importance. Children who are just beginning to read, whether they are telling the story in their own words or attempting to read the words on the page, look at the pictures a great deal for inspiration and reassurance. Pictures which look beautiful but do not match the text are distracting and confusing. Telling the story in their own words is one of the first steps in learning to read. Some children have good memories for words and can repeat the text of a simple story fairly accurately after hearing it only once or twice. Others catch the sense of the story without retaining the exact words. They, too, can 'read' the book because they can repeat the story. In one case it is the resonance of the words and in the other the understanding of the story or the ability to follow the sequence of the pictures which makes this very early reading possible. However the result is achieved, it shows just how important it is to start with the right text and pictures.

26 Picture books are the richest source of first books to read. For children who are involved in books the natural extension of hearing a story is to tell it, partly in their own words and partly in the words they remember. From there, they can begin to look at the words as they are printed and, again from memory, combined with their knowledge of letters and sounds, to read them. Memory plays an enormous part in this early stage. That is why looking at books and reading them aloud before they can read to themselves is so vital. Without that experience they will have nothing to remember and nothing to build on.

Some picture books are especially well suited to learning because their structure and therefore their vocabulary are repetitive. It may not be the repeated words themselves which make them easier to read, but the familiarity of the words and sounds is appealing in itself, which makes children want to go on with that book. In *Across the Stream* by Mirra Ginsburg and Nancy Tafuri, the hen and her chicks have a bad dream that the fox is after them. To escape, they cross the stream, 'a chick on a duckling, a chick on a duckling, a chick on a duckling and a hen on a duck'. Or there is Anne Rockwell's *Cars*, which gives one-line descriptions of different kinds of cars and what they do. 'Cars go everywhere.' 'There are big cars and small cars, old cars and new cars.' And so on. *Cars* is a book that works well for children (mostly boys, one has to say) who are already interested in cars because it gives them the words they are already familiar with in speech. The words of both these books gain strength from the very deliberate, almost rhythmic, use of repetition and this, combined with their illustrations which show exactly what the words are saying, makes them just right for learning to read.

Rhyme, too, can be a useful aid. The Dr Seuss books, such as *The Cat in the Hat* or *One Fish, Two Fish*, use all sorts of odd and zany words which make the books funny and unusual. Some of the words are too far-fetched to be useful but the knowledge that the word rhymes will make intelligent guessing, and then reading, come more easily.

If children are to enjoy learning to read and feel that it is worth the effort then they need books that they will respond to particularly. A gentle book like *My Cat Likes to Hide in Boxes* by Eve Sutton and Lynley Dodd tells of the things that cats from around the world may do: 'The cat from France likes to sing and dance', 'The cat from Norway got stuck in the doorway', and so on, all wittily illustrated and contrasting with *my* cosy cat who 'likes to hide in boxes'. The combination of fun and warmth is exactly right for some children. Others will be inspired by something more robust like the zany *Me and My Friend* by Allan Ahlberg and Colin McNaughton, which combines cartoon illustration and a jokey text in a cheery, easy-to-read book.

27

ME AND MY FRIEND

Choosing a book which keeps the reader engrossed is of paramount importance but the difficulties of learning to read do not end there. It is extremely hard to understand what makes reading easy for one child and a struggle for another. And because it is hard to understand it is very hard to help. Here are just two words of warning. Firstly, a simple vocabulary doesn't necessarily mean short words or the most common words. Children have just as much difficulty with 'and' or 'the' as they do with 'elephant' or 'banana'. Often they can remember the shape or structure of a complex word at least as easily as a simple one. Secondly, though a repetitive text may seem to be the obvious answer, children can be most disconcerting. They can read a word once on a page and then not recognise it the next time. They can even read it three or four times and then seem not to recognise it. For a reader this seems incomprehensible (and infuriating) but unless you know exactly how the child is 'reading' the word it is impossible to understand why they can read it once but not when they next see it or why they can read some words and not others.

The great thing is to stay calm. It is extremely difficult not to get impatient at best, and at worst angry, when this happens with your own child. But reading is very much a question of trial and error and you must be prepared to stand a lot of error if you are to help your child to learn.

Picture books are the first base of reading and will last for a long time. If apt and well chosen, the pictures start by being essential and then become a prop which may not be necessary but which many children like to have. Anything that helps give confidence that reading is possible at this early stage is vital. Even when children are reading books which are not strictly picture books they will want to go back to them – and should do so.

Learning to read does not just mean moving on to more and more difficult books and dropping the old ones. It is about enjoyment and entertainment. If a fluent reader wants to read a picture book, so be it. You should never say, 'That's a baby book. It's too easy for you.' A reader is someone who enjoys books, not someone who has reached a certain reading level.

As your child becomes more confident, the balance between picture and text can shift gradually. Knowing more words means they will not be daunted by longer texts. Pictures will still play an important part in both reading and enjoyment but the words themselves can convey more. Holding the reader's attention remains an essential factor. Because so much energy has to go into decoding the words the new reader finds it hard to concentrate on a complex story. This means that there is usually a substantial discrepancy between what the child can comprehend and what they can actually read. (This lasts until the child is a wholly fluent reader and remains a problem for the whole of that period.) It can be a particular difficulty for children who have been read good stories from the beginning – but don't let that stop you! The good done by reading aloud far outweighs any possible bad.

There are books which can combine interesting content and easily readable text, especially if they have something more to offer than a straightforward story. The comic adventures of the Berenstain bears, in such titles as *The Big Honey Hunt* or *Bears on Holiday*, by Stan and Jan Berenstain, provide some very good laughs. Their rhyming texts help with the guessing too. The exploits of Mrs Gaddy in Wilson Gage's *The Crow and Mrs Gaddy* and *Mrs Gaddy and the Fast-Growing Vine* also manage to be funny and easy to read. The storylines in both are quite strong enough to make a child want to go on reading.

Spooks and fear can be another way of gripping the reader while sticking to a simple text. In James Marshall's *Four On the Shore* a group of children tell each other scary stories and end up frightening the reader – and themselves. The whole concept is very child-centred so the reader is easily pulled right in. *In a Dark, Dark Room and Other Scary Stories*, by Alvin Schwartz and Dirk Zimmer, is a collection of seven horribly frightening stories, most simply written. The text in this, and all the other books in the I Can Read series, is large and clearly set on the page which also makes them look enticing.

The I Can Read series shows that just because books are in a series they do not have to be dreary or restricted. Arnold Lobel's Frog and Toad titles, Kay Choroa's *Oink and Pearl*, Nathaniel Benchley's *Red Fox and His Canoe* – all of these quite different stories are original and highly readable. They make a sharp contrast to the sometimes predictable and pedestrian books found in series and show how important it is to give the right book to the right child.

Series are a mixed blessing and a mixed bag. I Can Read is a particularly good one. And there are many others for all the stages from beginners to fluent readers – Cartwheels, Banana books, Jets,

29

Kites, and more. They are a useful and sensible marketing concept which helps identify the particular level of a book. Reading within a series gives reassurance to a child but it should be done carefully. Always pick out books on an individual basis, looking for good authors or good subjects, rather than just reaching for any old one. Sometimes the title itself will hook a reader. *The Chicken Pox Party* by Delia Huddy and *The Perfect Hamburger* by Alexander McCall Smith – titles such as these engage the reader and overcome any problems of boredom from the beginning. Choosing individually like this from a series will give much more satisfaction than can ever be achieved from a 'books by the yard' approach.

30

Remember, too, that many – even most – of the best stories are not in series. Their individual layout may make them look more difficult but the words they use are no harder (most series books, unless they are in a reading scheme, do not have a restricted vocabulary) and the stories are often fresher and more exhilarating. The restrictions on series books are more to do with length and concept than actual vocabulary. And it is just for these reasons that they can be dull. Ultimately, it is not the length of the book or its carefully chosen vocabulary which is important. The quality of the story is what counts. Ted Hughes's *The Iron Man*, which is an excellent book to read aloud from (see Chapter One), is also a surprisingly easy book to read. His choice of words is careful and unpretentious which means that the vocabulary is mostly simple. The brilliance of the story is encouragement enough to keep the child reading even if they need help with a few words. Good illustrations help too.

Choosing good books for the right stages will help develop a child's reading until suddenly, and usually surprisingly, it is happening. You or your child will be choosing *books*, regardless of any special categorisation, and the pleasure of reading will be established. Learning to read is a roundabout and gradual process, with lots of going backwards and forwards, and lots of stops and starts. At every point along the way the child will need help. Try to make the whole thing less daunting. Choose every book carefully but try to make it fun and not a chore. Making a child 'read' a totally unfamiliar book to you is very offputting. Suggest reading a book together, one page each, or one chapter each. Let the child read a book that they know, again and again, if they want to. This remains as important for the first books that they tackle on their own as it is for the earliest picture books they read, and remains important even when they seem to be able to read alone. Do anything that helps establish the pleasure of reading. And, above all, don't stop reading aloud just at the point when they can read to themselves. Reading alone and reading aloud are two different activities. They enhance rather than exclude each other.

This is an ideal model of how to help your child to learn to read. But, in practice, learning to read is far more complicated, as many parents know and many others will soon discover. The fact is that there is no foolproof way in which children learn to read. If there were, it could be used for all children and there would be no need for further discussion.

31

So what do you do when your child is finding it hard to learn to read? The first thing is not to panic. As a parent the most important thing is to have confidence that your child *will* learn to read and not to worry unduly about *when* they do so. Children are ready to read at different ages, just as they are ready to walk or talk at different ages. For some, it just 'clicks' and they move quickly and smoothly through the early stages. For many others, it is a slow and difficult process.

Learning to read is *the* big thing for most parents when their children start school. Whether or not their child can read is almost always a matter of anxiety and, if they are honest, of competition. There can be few primary-school parents who can put their hands on their hearts and say that they have never had a conversation about their child's reading prowess. Everyone knows that learning to read requires a brain and it is therefore all too easy to equate being able to do it, and do it young, with being intelligent. While most people would not know how to quantify mathematical ability, they all know – or think they know – how to test reading.

From the day they start school, there is pressure on children to learn to read. Many parents may even have suggested to their children that school is for 'learning to read and write'. The first steps in learning to read may be the first direct teaching outside the home that a child receives. At schools where enormous emphasis is put on learning to read, *not* reading may be their first experience of failure.

Interestingly, the definition of a reader is not as concrete as might be expected. Is a swimmer someone who swims with armbands, someone who swims with one toe on the bottom or someone who swims freely? Is a reader the child who can struggle through a text with adult prompting and correction or the child who can settle down quietly on their own with a book and follow the story without help? The answer is that both are readers if they think they are. Given confidence, the struggling beginner will soon become an experienced free reader. Some competitive parents insist that their child can read when it is actually doing little more than 'barking at print'. Other parents deny that the child can read because they are not confident solo readers and they find it hard to see that the one is an important step towards the other. Both positions are extreme because many parents don't know enough about how reading happens.

Teachers are much better judges of a child's reading. A teacher can often see that a child can read while the parent swears that they cannot. Knowing more about how reading happens, teachers recognise that the child has reached a particular stage in learning to read while all the parent can see is that the child still needs help with every third word.

Parents are rightly encouraged to help their children by listening to their reading at home. But this apparently simple activity is extremely difficult in practice. Most parents find helping a child learn to read very, very hard. The suggestion is that it is an easy and natural thing to do, but it is not. It requires infinite patience and a great deal of time, two commodities which are usually in short supply with other small children about. It also requires more knowledge of some of the technicalities than most parents possess. Should you sound letters to help the child? Should you correct the child if they have got the word almost right but not quite? Is getting the sense of the story more important than being word-perfect on the actual text? All these things depend on what the child is being taught at school and on how they respond to learning.

Parents' attitudes to reading can play a significant part in a child's approach. Reading can be acquired as a 'notched-up' skill or for a purpose. Learning to read can be a separate task, detached from the enjoyable activity of reading, or it can be absorbed gradually through an involvement in books which starts as a baby and which is shown by parental example to be equally enjoyed as an adult. How books are treated at home will affect which approach a child will adopt.

The first two chapters of this book show how books can be used with babies from the very earliest age and the importance of reading aloud. These two activities are the backbone of learning to read. Familiarity with a book means that long before a child can decipher individual letters, long before they can speak clearly or articulate precisely, they know how a book is shaped. They understand that you move through a book, even if they don't know which is the right way up. Gradually, they learn to differentiate between the words and the pictures, and see that they are two separate parts of a whole. At a later stage still, the reader's finger moving under the print shows the child different words, different letter sounds. Knowing this basic structure of a book is an important step towards learning to read.

33

The importance of reading aloud is two-fold. In overall terms it gives the child an idea of what books contain, and a child who has heard good stories will understand why it is worth learning to read. The second advantage is more specific. It is enormously hard to read words which you have never heard. Unless the reader is a demon at phonic pronunciation (and even then English has a way of foxing you) it is extremely hard to work out exactly how a written word should sound. A child who has been read to will have developed a very large vocabulary. They will have heard words which are often used on paper but rarely in speech. And not only will they know how a word sounds, they will almost certainly have asked what it means or picked up this information from its context in a sentence.

But what if you have done all that? What if the parental attitude has been a positive one? Why is it that some children still find learning to read so very hard? There are many parents who have done everything mentioned above and in other chapters but whose children still find learning to read a slow and laborious process. (I know this from experience because my own children have varied wildly in their aptitude for reading despite having had almost exactly the same exemplary (!) pre-reading experiences.)

This is especially irritating in a situation where other parents tell you smugly that their children have learnt to read because they have had such good examples held before them ('We both read so much, you know'), because they have been read to so much ('I've always read to them ever since they were babies'), because – unstated – they are so clever. The simple answer is that the main ingredient in learning to read is the child. Every child is different and so there will be a great many responses to learning to read, and most of them will not follow a tidy, pre-structured path.

One of the other difficulties about learning to read lies in the assumption that all children should be ready to start reading at the same time. There is no magic moment at which reading should begin. It is always tied to starting school but the age for that varies from country to country. When first offered reading some children are not ready to concentrate for long enough or hard enough. Some have genuine difficulty in distinguishing between letters. There is a strongly held, but hard to prove, belief that boys – in general – find learning to read more difficult than girls. Whatever the cause, children are ready to read at different times and until they have some desire to learn they will find the whole process difficult and unrewarding. Too much emphasis on reading at the wrong time may be more damaging than beneficial.

When in despair about your child's inability to read, it is worth remembering the long-term reason for learning to read. Just because a child finds the learning hard it does not mean that they will ultimately be a worse reader. All the good preparation may not have made the decoding of print faster or easier but the chances are that once the child *has* learnt to read, they will be eager and motivated to do so. In the long run it is actually better to be a happy, enthusiastic reader than an early one. There are no statistics to prove that real readers are made young. The message for the parent is 'have confidence'. Go on reading aloud, looking at picture books, listening to their reading patiently. Don't worry if progress is slow and not very steady. In the end, only a handful of children entirely fail to learn to read.

Reading is a vital skill. It is vital for discovering and understanding the world and it is the key to a massive storehouse of entertainment. Children who do not learn to read will always be at an enormous disadvantage. They do not need to learn especially young and they do not need to learn in a particular way. They may use reading as a tool for finding out or they may use it to take themselves to a different world. As your child struggles or sails towards acquiring the skill, remember that the end product should be a *real* reader.

FURTHER READING

No ages have been given for these books. The time at which they are suitable will depend on the individual child.

ALLAN AHLBERG *Mrs Plug the Plumber*, illustrated by Janet Ahlberg, Puffin

This is just one of the witty, easy-to-read stories in the Happy Families series. In this story Mrs Plug earns the money plumbing while Mr Plug stays at home to mind the babies. Her tools enable her to stop a robbery which leads to a lovely reward – a luxury cruise for the family. When the boat springs a leak, who better to help than – Mrs Plug? Ridiculous, original stories make this book and the others in the series the best possible kind of entertainment.

SHIRLEY HUGHES *Chips and Jessie*, Fontana

Shirley Hughes has broken across barriers of classification in this imaginatively and intelligently devised book. Strip cartoons, pictures and text, continuous text – each of the tiny stories in this book is told in a different way. All revolve around two friends, Chips and Jessie, and their dog and cat. The text is light and the illustrations humorous. The strip cartoons entice readers in and then encourage them to persevere with the continuous text.

PRISCILLA LAMONT *The Troublesome Pig*, Piper

The strong rhythm and repetitive text of this familiar rhyme make it a good book to practise reading on. The pig won't jump over the stile and so, in desperation, the old woman calls on one animal after another to help her. The pig's stubbornness, her despair and the attempts to get him to jump are all illustrated in soft watercolours which are both beautiful and funny. The text may look daunting but it contains many repetitions.

PHOEBE and SELBY WORTHINGTON *Teddy Bear Coalman*, Puffin

Deeply old-fashioned but nonetheless charming, this is a day in the life of a teddy bear coalman. The text is basic: 'This is the story of

Teddy Bear Coalman. He had a horse, a cart and three little bags of coal.' It is closely illustrated so that the child can easily guess the words just by looking at the pictures. We follow the teddy bear coalman on his rounds, so there is a lot of repeated text as he delivers the coal or clip-clops down the road between customers.

ACTION AND ADVENTURE

CHAPTER FOUR

FICTION GIVES READERS a chance to play any manner of roles both in their own and in different worlds. All the business of learning to read will be rewarded by the delight of getting 'lost in a book'. Stories offer many kinds of entertainment. They provide reassurance with familiar images and situations and they also provoke thought and experimentation by taking children into new worlds.

It is not the extent of the gulf between the real and the imaginary that makes good fiction. 'Real life' stories, which can be subdivided into family stories, animal stories, adventure stories, school stories and historical stories, can be just as inventive as fantasy and science fiction novels set in brave new worlds. Good fiction of any kind contains two key ingredients – a convincing character or characters to identify with, and a strong plot which, by its effective use of anxiety, excitement or whatever, will make the reader go on reading. These two elements determine whether a story is really good or merely passable. In different kinds of stories the balance between plot and character varies, and other factors, such as the details of setting, the technicalities of another lifestyle or the strength of the relationships, become important too.

Family stories are usually structured around an adventure or drama for the sake of readability, but it is the credibility of the characters and the unveiling of emotions which make the book distinctive. All children need these kinds of stories because they offer reassurance about the things that happen to them and their own home lives. Sometimes readers can see themselves in the domestic situations described in the book so they can empathise with the characters and learn from their reactions. At other times the experiences are beyond their own, in which case they can learn through identifying with the convincing fictional characters' reaction to them.

Betsy Byars's *The Eighteenth Emergency* revolves around the timid 'Mouse' who spends much of his time planning how to cope with seventeen imaginary emergencies but finds it hard to cope when the eighteenth arrives in the all too real form of a school bully. Mouse's predicament is a familiar one to many children and Betsy Byars handles a potentially frightening situation with sympathy and understanding, while her witty style enables her to make a serious point lightly.

The unusual, highly original and very funny solution to a broken marriage that lies at the heart of *Madame Doubtfire*, by Anne Fine, provides a way of looking at some of the things that children, especially when they are very young, find particularly hard to take about their parents' separation. Anne Fine lets us laugh as Dad pretends to be the housekeeper and the children go through the elaborate charade of knowing him and yet not knowing him. But she leaves us in no doubt about the suffering which this confused situation causes.

More soberly, *Bridge to Terabithia* is a profoundly moving story about how Jess feels when her best friend Leslie is killed in a terrible accident while playing their special game. Katherine Paterson avoids slush but she does not pull her punches. This story forces children to think about friendship and death, the last being especially important since it is not commonly touched on in children's fiction.

Each of these three books takes on a major issue. The first is common to all children since they will all experience bullying of one kind or another in their lives. The other two are specific incidents which most children will never encounter personally. Without obvious didacticism these excellent fictional accounts give insights into unusual aspects of 'ordinary' life which concern children, whether they are directly involved or not, and which are rarely discussed openly.

Most family stories are less cataclysmic but equally important. They deal with domestic upheavals such as moving house and leaving friends or changing schools. Or, still less dramatically, they offer fictional situations which mirror life and, in so doing, comfort and reassure. Beverly Cleary's Ramona books capture the tiny ups and downs in the life of the little girl Ramona, her oldest sister, Mum, Dad and the cat Picky-Picky. From the first title, *Ramona the Pest*, and on through all the others about the same family, Beverly Cleary shows how a six-year-old views life. She has absolute understanding of the mixed emotions on starting school or the unhappiness of staying with a minder until Mum is free. In *Colvin and the Snake Basket*, Sam McBratney shows the same understanding of Colvin, a middle child who feels himself unluckily placed between his bossy older sister, Beccy, and the baby, Frederick, who is young enough to do as he wishes and get away with it.

Books in which animals play a central role are either animal adventures which look at life through an animal's eyes or, more commonly, stories about a child and a pet. Many children long for pets; fewer parents want them. The idea that owning a pet gives you something to love and care for, and – underlying this – something to love you back, is a strong one. All children who have had to beg, plead and nag for a pet will understand exactly how much the gerbils Bubble and Squeak mean to Sid, Peggy and Amy in *The Battle of Bubble and Squeak* by Philippa Pearce. Even when the pets are safely owned there is still the problem of Mum, who would do anything (almost) to get rid of them. The battle is between the children and Mum, and the gerbils are at the centre of it. But when the neighbour's cat plays its part and the gerbils' lives are in danger, it is Mum who saves them. This is an exceptional animal story which also looks closely at family dynamics.

National Velvet by Enid Bagnold is a wildly improbable story which is credible almost despite itself. Velvet is fourteen and horse-mad. She rides and grooms an imaginary horse until she wins The Piebald in a raffle. Such is her commitment and belief that the reader, too, can easily follow her on her triumphant Grand National win – disguised as a boy. This is a girl's fantasy about a horse which far exceeds even the wildest dreams of girls in pony stories. It works because we are never for a moment allowed to think that it will not.

For an animal adventure with only a small, though very evil, human element, Dodie Smith's *One Hundred and One Dalmatians* is hard to beat. Pongo and Missis are desperate to save their pups from the clutches of the dreaded Cruella de Vil who has stolen them to make spotted gloves and coats. The puppies are saved in a tense and dramatic rescue operation organised and executed entirely by dogs.

39

The success of a plot often depends on the adventure at its core. A book is a form of escape from everyday life, so even when the story can broadly be described as 'real' it will be full of the kind of adventures which just don't seem to happen in real life. Their credibility comes instead from the author's ability to tell them well. There are many well-established conventions in this kind of children's book. Parents are frequently removed early on so that the children can have free rein. Without adults present, the children have to make decisions and cope according to their own judgement. Even quite simple situations can appear complicated when there is no adult at hand – though the adults can often be brought back at a suitable moment, either a moment of triumph for the children or when the situation becomes desperate. Arthur Ransome's *Swallows and Amazons* and all his subsequent titles about the same children and their boats are a clever combination of children acting on their own but from a secure basis. Things can go wrong but not disastrously so, and many children would like to emulate the delicious freedom and independence of the *Swallows and Amazons* children as they sail in the Lake District.

The idea of a group or gang operating together is part of the adventure tradition, from the most widely known gang books of all – Enid Blyton's Famous Five series – to Cynthia Voight's masterly *Homecoming*, one of the best books of recent years. *Homecoming* tells the story of a family of four children travelling across America in search of relatives who will take them in, after their mentally unstable mother has abandoned them in a car park. There are few major incidents, though many minor ones, in this long and totally compulsive book, but the daily interaction of the children, the way they help each other, react to stress, fall apart and then just keep on going is quite enough action in itself. In both these examples, and in many other stories of the same kind, there is an optimistic or idealistic view of children's ability to work together. In children's fiction they usually do, give or take the odd disagreement. William Golding has an interestingly different scenario in *The Lord of the Flies* which runs against this tradition.

Mystery-solving often provides the plot for this kind of fiction. In reality, few children ever discover anything really mysterious in their lives but nevertheless the search for smugglers, spies, treasure or secrets of one sort or another is a common enough theme. In recent years, mysteries have become more topical. There have been several novels for older children about the well-kept secrets of nuclear missiles and the dumping of nuclear waste. Two successful books of this kind are Robert Swindells's *The Serpent's Tooth* and James Watson's *Where Nobody Sees*. In both, the teenage characters are involved in passionate campaigning against the use of local land for anything that might be potentially dangerous or contaminating. Bureaucracy and money-making also come in for a bashing. Stories like this, which make points about social changes, play an important and educative role while retaining all the conventions of fiction. They show just how far the concept of mystery or adventure fiction can be extended.

Adventure stories have a reputation for being unliterary. Too much reliance on plot or high drama can be absurd, unconvincing and convention-bound. But the best adventure stories are nothing of the sort. They use the drama and excitement of an adventure with subtlety so that the story holds the reader's attention without ever becoming melodramatic, even though the action may have to be a little larger than life. Nina Bawden tells stories of this kind. The action of *Rebel on the Rock* takes place on a Greek island where Charlie and Jo are all set to have an idle and rather dull holiday. Instead they get caught up in a revolutionary war and all that it entails. Like many of Nina Bawden's other books, this is a story full of drama – an adventure story. It holds its audience because it is so well written and because the characters, in the roles they play, are convincing.

41

High drama, melodrama and dramatic accidents are rare in real life, but in fiction they not only create tension and add a touch of glamour, they also break the pattern of life for the fictional characters, thus giving them a chance to look at things anew. This also allows the reader to consider things from a different angle. One of the most spectacular fictional accidents is Katy's fall from the swing in *What Katy Did* by Susan Coolidge. This event changes the wild and headstrong Katy into someone considerably tamer and more cautious. Other accidents or illnesses are less dramatic but they similarly enable the characters to step outside their normal lives for a while.

Family stories and animal stories show that adventures can occur in any setting. The difference lies in the balance between the action and the characters. Where adventure stories depend on the plot for their success, family stories and animal stories rely on the interaction of characters – human and human, human and animal, or animal and animal.

In the other two main areas of 'real' fiction, school and historical stories, setting is added to character and plot becomes the distinguishing factor. School provides an obvious background. It is familiar and it can be easily and amusingly embellished. The school story tradition is a long one, and has its roots in the self-contained worlds of private boarding schools. Schools such as Linbury Court where Jennings and Derbyshire play leading roles in the wilder activities of the boarders in the Jennings books starting with *Jennings Goes to School*, by Anthony Buckeridge, the very specialist choir school world of William Mayne's *A Swarm in May*, Antonia Forest's Kingscote where from *Autumn Term* onwards the Marlowe family follow one another in order to shine in every possible area, the Chalet school set amid the beautiful Swiss countryside, Anne Digby's Trebizon – all of these are solidly and convincingly created. School story addicts know them intimately and for them no series can ever be too long.

School lends itself particularly well to adventure for many reasons. It is a completely enclosed world with its own culture and mores. The parents are removed and the teachers have a distant and largely negative role. Avoiding them adds the excitement of defiance and the spice of possible discovery. The children inevitably form gangs so that there is both the delight of group activity and the danger of inter-gang warfare. Thrills are easy to manufacture because doing almost anything means breaking the rules and therefore running the risk of punishment. The strangest fact about stories of this kind is that they have always appealed as much to children who did *not* go to such schools as to those who did. For outsiders, there is the urge to satisfy their curiosity about a private world. For the insider, the nature of the appeal is more complex because they are able to laugh at and with the jokes.

If the origins of the school story lie in boarding schools, more recent stories have been firmly set in local primary or comprehensive schools. The Grange Hill series, created by Phil Redmond for television and adapted as a series of books by Robert Leeson in titles such as *Grange Hill Rules, OK?*, has come to epitomise a comprehensive school. It is seen as absolutely archetypal by a few children and by many parents. Gene Kemp, an ex-teacher herself, has a sure eye for the background details of school and Cricklepit Primary provides a secure and convincing setting for *The Turbulent Term of Tyke Tiler*. Bernard Ashley, a primary-school headmaster, uses his intimate knowledge of school, and the central role it plays in many children's lives, as significant background for his urban stories, such as *Taller than Before*. The things that happen at Joan Smith's Pepper Street Primary seem as real as those in one's own school because she has picked out the salient features of school life and describes exactly how the children interact on major occasions such as the school nativity play in *We Three Kings From Pepper Street Prime*.

By revising and updating its setting, the school story has retained its central position in mainstream fiction. Historical fiction, which also uses background as an important ingredient, cannot do this. Because it is set in the past, historical fiction has never had either the advantages or disadvantages of being topical. It is always in its own time and whether it works or not depends on the author's skill at recreating that world and time for the reader. Historical fiction has long been of an exceptional quality but, sadly, the demand for it among contemporary children is declining, with the result that there are few new writers of the genre. Like any other kind of fiction, it must have convincing characters and an engrossing drama. In addition, it has to set these in a credible time past. This must be done with great delicacy. Too much historical detail and the book can feel as if it has been written from a card index; too little, and it becomes merely a costume drama in which the characters are contemporary except for their trappings.

43

Rosemary Sutcliff is a writer of rare gifts. She creates convincing characters and tells dramatic stories, and her re-creation of the past seems almost effortless. Her historical settings carry a conviction which makes them far more telling and memorable than any number of history lessons because she looks at the domestic as well as the dramatic side of the past. In *Warrior Scarlet* the young boy Drem overhears a conversation about himself. His mother is weaving scarlet cloth on the loom, ready for the day when he has slain a wolf singlehanded and so become a warrior of the tribe. But his grandfather is less optimistic. He makes no bones about his belief that Drem, with his withered arm, will never kill a wolf and will have to go and live as a shepherd. The anger, self-pity and pain which Drem feels when he hears this, and his desperate need to go away and hide, are as intense as the almost unbearable excitement when he fails to kill the wolf, or the very different, quieter drama when he finally does kill his wolf in quite other circumstances. In all her books set in any historical period – and she has covered many, though Roman Britain most extensively – Rosemary Sutcliff brings the past to life as a real time when real people lived.

There are other writers who also have this particular ability to take their readers into the past. Henry Treece's Viking trilogy, starting with *Viking's Dawn*, revolves around Harald Sigurdson, a Norse boy who joins the crew of a Viking longship as it sets out on a voyage of discovery and plunder. The fine writing recreates the atmosphere of the time as well as describing incidents vividly.

Geoffrey Trease's interest in history has led him to write more than fifty novels set in the past. His first book, *Bows Against the Barons*, was a vivid retelling of the Robin Hood story, with Robin shown very much as a friend of the poor with strong egalitarian beliefs. More recently, in *Tomorrow is a Stranger*, he describes what life was like in Guernsey when the Germans occupied it during the Second World War. He tells the story from the children's point of view, showing how completely their world changed during the Occupation – not least because the adults started to tell lies. With this kind of observation of the domestic changes as well as the sweeping changes in society as a whole, he gives the reader a chance to live then too.

Less wide-ranging in period and subject-matter, but with the same ability to bring the past to life, is Gillian Avery. Her books have late Victorian settings and a wholly domestic flavour, but show how strong, independent girls operated in a society which offered them little room to flourish. *The Warden's Niece*, which starts with Maria's dramatic escape from her horrendous school, is the most completely satisfying because it has the best constructed plot. It also contains a very memorable character – Mr Copplestone, the tall, eccentric tutor.

These are established writers who have been writing for the last half century. Among the few new writers of historical fiction is Julian Atterton. He has written highly readable historical novels, both for younger readers in *The Shape-Changer*, a Viking story of love and magic, and for teenagers in *The Tournament of Fortune*, a fast-paced, romantic story set in England during the reign of Edward II. Philip Pullman, another new writer, may not be so committed to the historical genre but in *The Ruby in the Smoke* he gives a powerful and atmos-

44

pheric impression of London and the changing fashions, occupations and new technologies of the late Victorian period.

The apparent lack of interest in historical fiction may be partly due to teenagers being more concerned about what is going on now in the world around them or it may be because they are more introspective. Perhaps while there is doubt about the future of the world there is less inclination to worry about the past. For whatever reason, it will be a major loss if a great fictional tradition is allowed to die. Then again, maybe the decline in historical fiction will be compensated for by a move towards brilliant and inventive historical fantasies such as those written by Joan Aiken. The wholly invented world of *The Wolves of Willoughby Chase* has a strong historical flavour. Without being set in a 'real' historical period it gives a feeling for the past and thus makes a highly successful bridge between the best kind of historical writing and the best in the fiction of the 'unreal' world too.

45

FURTHER READING

LOUISE FITZHUGH *Harriet the Spy*, Fontana

Harriet is curious about people, so curious that she becomes a spy. In her secret notebook she writes, 'I'm a spy that writes down everything.' Her observations are ruthless, shrewd and sometimes cruel. She is accused of snooping but her thirst for information is quite genuine. Louise Fitzhugh has written an unusual book that gives an authentic child's view of the world. (10+)

JUDITH KERR *When Hitler Stole Pink Rabbit*, Fontana

Anna and her family flee from Nazi Germany with almost no possessions. Their comfortable, wealthy life in Germany is over and they must start a new, hard life as refugees. Judith Kerr's story is autobiographical but she tells it without rancour. Instead it is a charming and good-humoured account of a family in distress but ever hopeful. (9+)

JILL PATON WALSH *Gaffer Sampson's Luck*, Puffin

Newly arrived in a tightly knit village, James finds himself an outsider as far as the other children are concerned. He makes friends with Gaffer Sampson, the old, bedridden man next door, who needs James's help to find his missing 'luck'. James's search for the 'luck' leads him to accept a dangerous and silly dare from the village children. Jill Paton Walsh attracts the reader with her sympathetic central character and his convincing relationship with the other children and Gaffer Sampson, and holds us with the tautness of the plot.　　(9+)

FAY SAMPSON *A Free Man on Sunday*, Gollancz

46　　Set in 1932, *A Free Man on Sunday* describes an episode of recent British social history which sounds as if it comes from the Dark Ages. The Mass Trespass on Kinder Scout is organised in an effort to prevent the hills and moors of the north of England being closed off as game reserves for the very rich. Edie has been brought up to spend her weekends rambling with her father but he forbids her to join him on this particular Sunday. She defies her father and joins him on the Trespass which was intended as a peaceful demonstration but becomes violent and dangerous, especially for Edie and her father.　　(10+)

A. RUTGERS VAN DER LOEFF *Children on the Oregon Trail*, Puffin

Though only the length of an ordinary book, *Children on the Oregon Trail* is a saga. The terrible hardships of the long, long journey westwards across America in the last century are spelt out clearly in this story of a pioneer family's trek to a better life. There are endless dangers, such as swollen rivers too wide to cross safely and warlike Indians, as well as shortage of food and the ravages of disease. The resilience and bravery of the children, who must, in the end, continue their journey alone, is both exciting and deeply moving.　　(10+)

MAGIC
AND MYSTICISM
CHAPTER FIVE

LONGSIDE STORIES OF the real world there are all the superb stories set in unreal places of one kind or another. These novels are set in worlds far away from our own – in the future, on different planets, in ghostly or in wholly imaginary worlds. Books of this kind have a licence to invent that is missing from 'real' stories. The authors can create a whole new land and people it accordingly. Alternatively, space fiction novels can blend our own time and place with the brave new world of space either by bringing visitors to Earth or by sending humans hurtling out into space.

Fiction for younger readers is peppered with stories about aliens coming to Earth. One example is Jane who comes to stay for a two-week holiday with Katy and her family in Sheila Lavelle's *The Apple Pie Alien*. Like many such aliens she has odd features and causes havoc because they do things differently out there. In *The Blue Misty Monsters* the Mistys come to Earth from outer space and take a pretty dim view of us 'Two-Leggers' whom they regard as rather primitive. Catherine Sefton uses the book to make some sharp observations about our patterns of behaviour, while writing in a light and humorous way. In Robin Klein's *Halfway Across the Galaxy*, X and her family are programmed to arrive in eighteenth-century Versailles. Instead they end up rather at a loss in the present day. They, too, make shrewd observations about many of the things which we take for granted.

Our increased knowledge of space has also led to speculation about the possibility of living on other planets or in space stations. The novels that do this are more technical than those that feature little space aliens coming to Earth. They expect the reader to delight in the technology of computers and lasers and to follow discussions about gravity and other scientific concepts. Often they use the new planet or our own planet in a future time as a background against which to test conventional morality or to make statements about the freedom of the individual or the value of democracy. At their best they are idealistic and creative. At their worst they offer stereotypes, especially of male domination.

Monica Hughes has written a number of excellent space fiction novels in which she has tackled these themes in a variety of ways. For her Isis trilogy she created the planet Isis, ruled by the beautiful girl, Olwen, who has been horribly changed so as to survive in the strange atmosphere. *The Keeper of the Isis Light* and its two sequels make the idea of living on another planet seem perfectly plausible. The attraction of this kind of fiction is that all the rules are still being made and the setting can be as fanciful as the author wishes. Douglas Hill's ColSec novels, starting with *Exiles of ColSec*, are set in the future when the dropouts of society are put into a malfunctioning space craft and sent to their deaths. In this case a group of kids manages to land on Klydor, a habitable planet, and to survive despite their own violent natures and the inhospitable character of the other occupants. Douglas Hill's hard-edged writing vividly combines life on a new planet with swashbuckling acts of heroism and laser battles between goodies and baddies.

48

Space fiction can seem safely futuristic and imaginary. More threatening and more thought-provoking are the books which take a look at our own society as it might be in the not too distant future. Fictional speculation of this kind has many famous predecessors – George Orwell's *1984*, most obviously. (Fortunately, none of the more alarming predictions have come true – quite!) *The White Mountains* and the other two titles in the Tripods trilogy by John Christopher pose questions about one man's control of another and especially about freedom of thought. They are set in a time when individual thoughts are threatened by the Tripods, whose intention is to 'cap' people's heads so that their actions can be controlled by the Master. Resistance comes from a determined band of fugitives who survive and save the day. Slightly dated and full of male domination, the Tripods is still a series which blends drama and message in an exciting and easily readable narrative. Nicholas Fisk's *A Rag, a Bone and a Hank of Hair* is also about the control of people in a futuristic society. After a nuclear disaster Brin is one of the few survivors. He has the task of controlling the artificially created children on whom the future survival of the human race depends, and the book gives a disturbing insight into the most extreme possibilities of human engineering.

All these types of fiction use particular settings and hypothetical situations to air important and very real issues in an apparently unreal framework. For both writers and readers, fantasy has many of the same attractions as science fiction. It is a more elastic genre because it does not need to worry about scientific practicalities or possibilities. Fantasy has always attracted some of the very best writers, and their readers demand the highest standards of writing and creativity. C. S. Lewis's Narnia is probably the best-known and one of the most memorable fantasy worlds. The children's discovery of it – through a wardrobe in *The Lion, the Witch and the Wardrobe* – is memorable for its simplicity and because it gives all children the opportunity to believe that they might find such a world during their own games of hide and seek. Once in Narnia, the division between good and evil is clearly spelt out. The glittering evil of the White Witch, the simple goodness of Mr Tumnus and the overpowering control of Aslan are all easily assimilated. (The heavy Christian symbolism may worry adults but it is cheerfully unrecognised by children.) The choices are not hard for young readers to make, and they can afford to despise Edmund for making the wrong one.

49

Narnia is a fantasy kingdom and the battle is between the forces of good and evil. Earthsea, the setting of Ursula Le Guin's Earthsea trilogy, which begins with *The Wizard of Earthsea*, is similarly a whole fantasy world of wizards, or Archmadges, and dragons. And again there is a struggle between good and evil. Duny is a wild young boy who is no ordinary boy. Under his true name, Ged, he becomes an apprentice madge and finally Sparrowhawk, dragonlord and Archmadge. Moving from Ged's introduction to magic at the hands of his aunt through his testing apprenticeship to the gentle Ogion, *The Wizard of Earthsea* is a bit like following a magic course oneself since the points are so finely and carefully made. Ged is a captivating character and Ursula Le Guin immediately involves the reader with her detailed observation of life in the wizards' school, as seen through Ged's eyes.

The intensity of this magical world is at its simplest and best in *The Wizard of Earthsea*. The detailed creation of a fantasy world and the use of a special, spell-binding language is flawless. There is little plot to manage, so all the author's and reader's energies are concentrated on the characters, the setting and the moods. The sequels move into fantasy on a grander scale. The quest for the lost Ring of Erreth-Akbe lies at the heart of *The Tombs of Atuan*, and the loss of magic in Earthsea and Sparrowhawk's bold venture into the land of the dead dominates *The Farthest Shore*. Sparrowhawk the Archmadge is still a beguiling figure but he has lost the absolute appeal of his younger self, Ged.

Even more than Narnia or Earthsea, Middle Earth, the setting for J. R. R. Tolkien's *The Lord of the Rings*, is a kingdom which invites readers to enter in and immerse themselves completely. (In the 1960s the Tolkien cult was so strong that for many teenagers, especially in America, Middle Earth became more real than the planet Earth.) It is also a story of a violent battle between the forces of good and evil. The main plot of the three books in *The Lord of the Rings* centres on the Ring which carries the power of ruling. As in the Narnia books, there is heavy symbolism both in the story and in the elves, dwarfs and wizards which populate it. There is too much symbolism for some and too much suspension of disbelief for others. Where Ursula Le Guin's writing is light and magical, Tolkien's is heavy and solemn. His stories are long, slow and very well crafted. Neither in style nor plot are they to be taken lightly. They make such demands on the reader that you either love them or hate them.

On as massive a scale as *The Lord of the Rings* or the Earthsea trilogy (fantasies seem to take a lot of words to unfold) is Susan Cooper's *The Dark is Rising* sequence. This sequence consists of five books, starting with *Over Sea, Under Stone*, each of which is complete in itself while also forming a series of interrelated continuous adventures. Like the Narnia books, *The Dark is Rising* has real children as the main characters in the story. Unlike the others, though, the action is set in our own world with forces and characters from other worlds creeping in. Susan Cooper's books work because of her ability to blend the real and the unreal so that the reader can move fluently between the two. The good and evil theme lies at the heart of a great many fantasies (Susan Cooper's among them). Like science fiction, fantasy is an excellent forum in which to raise such issues, since the distancing from reality allows moral judgements to take on the resonance of universal truth instead of sounding like a criticism of certain individuals or kinds of regimes.

But these giant canvases are only one kind of fantasy. Others are more domestic. The individual, rather than a complete world, is affected by the fantasy or magic; it is something more internal, in the mind. In *A Dog So Small* Ben's yearning for a dog is so powerful that, when disappointed after being given a wool picture of a dog instead of the real thing, he creates a dog of his own. With his eyes screwed up tight he can 'see' his dog. But, with his eyes screwed up, he crosses the road and is knocked down by a car. The accident finally proves the extent of Ben's desperation for a dog and the story ends happily with the family moving and Ben getting a real puppy at last. Philippa Pearce shows how completely entwined the real and the imaginary worlds are for children. Recognising the sharp distinction between the two is one of the marks of growing up.

51

Magic or imagination – something impossible to specify – may be an important ingredient for individuals creating their own fantasies. *Emlyn's Moon* by Jenny Nimmo is a story of a family's break-up which is put right by a child's belief in the curative powers of magic and fantasy. The story is conveyed as much through mood as detail. The powers of magic are never exactly spelt out but the character's belief in them is wholly credible. A similar kind of fantasy is brilliantly displayed in John Burningham's *John Patrick Norman McHennessy – The Boy who was Always Late*, a picture book for older readers which makes a wonderful joke out of a child's different and outrageous reasons for being late for school. The final twist of the teacher's excuse adds an especially witty touch.

Blending imagination, fantasy and reality requires faultless control and great originality. The use of a time slip to take the characters into another world or to swap them with other people is often a successful, though usually less psychologically satisfying, device. Penelope Farmer employs it to excellent effect in *Charlotte Sometimes*, a story about a girl who finds herself changing places with the girl who occupied the same school bed many years previously.

Time slips may be fantasy or they may be ghostly. The idea of being haunted by the past is usually spine-chilling and sinister; ghosts

JOHN PATRICK NORMAN MCHENNESSY –
THE BOY WHO WAS ALWAYS LATE

have a bad reputation in fiction. Collections of ghost stories abound, ranging from the most horrible, like the world-famous *The Hound of the Baskervilles* by Arthur Conan Doyle, to more humorous spookings. Real ghost stories are a particular taste which I don't enjoy, except for some obviously light-hearted ones such as *The Haunting of Cassie Palmer* by Vivien Alcock. Cassie, the seventh child of a seventh child, tries to reject the beliefs of her mother who is a moderately successful medium. But then Cassie *is* haunted. Or is she? Vivien Alcock turns this story into a game which takes the fright out of it without removing the tension.

Much more chilling but still safely on the right side of a traditional ghost story is *The Changeover* by Margaret Mahy. Its spookiness comes not from rattling bones or unearthly shrieks but from something far more tangible – the belief that there is a spirit world which is just a little outside us all. When Jacko is critically ill, Laura is forced to work with the supernatural powers in order to save his life. Margaret Mahy allows us to move freely from one world to another. She convinces us that there are supernatural forces which affect us all, and in so doing she gives a new dimension to fiction.

Lois Duncan writes thrillers whose special twist is the psychic powers or supernatural qualities of her characters. *The Eyes of Karen Connors* tells the story of Karen whose 'third eye' enables her to see into the future. She fights hard to hide her special power but when a little child's life is at risk she cannot deny her 'sight' and uses it to resolve a hideous drama. Like Margaret Mahy, Lois Duncan's own belief in these extra senses impels us to believe in them too.

Ghosts, supernatural forces, flying saucers or strange and distant kingdoms – all of these are excellent sources of imaginative and thought-provoking stories. Well removed from the problems of daily life, they provide exactly the kind of escapism which many children look for in reading.

53

FURTHER READING

ROBIN CHAMBERS *The Ice Warrior and Other Stories*, illustrated by Julek Heller, Puffin

How can a long-dead footballer play in the World Cup? This unreal – impossible – happening lies at the heart of the title story in this powerful collection of four stories in which science fiction, supernatural and natural worlds are skilfully and easily blended together. Robin Chambers's writing is direct and forceful. His imagination is vivid and frightening. (9+)

ALAN GARNER *The Owl Service*, Fontana

Three children are trapped in an old Welsh legend and they must live through its ancient jealousies, fierce passions and powerful hatreds. Alan Garner's belief in this kind of pull from the past makes his story entirely credible while his gift for storytelling and his particular way of looking at the interaction between people give *The Owl Service* very special qualities. (10+)

PAT O'SHEA *The Hounds of the Morrigan*, Puffin

The crux of this long but fast-moving and highly readable fantasy is the coming of the Morrigan, the Great Queen, whose mission is to destroy the world. Two children, Pidge and Brigit, have been chosen to thwart the Queen's evil plan and they are greatly helped by people and things that are good and true. Thus good fights evil, but in the very lightest of ways. (10+)

LYNNE REID BANKS *The Indian in the Cupboard*, Fontana

When Omri puts his tiny toy American Indian figure into the cupboard for safekeeping it comes to life and there is a perfect miniature Indian Chief for him to play with. Omri looks forward to the adventures they can have together but Little Bull is no longer a toy. He has his own life into which Omri is drawn. Lynne Reid Banks has constructed an exquisite world in miniature. Her Indians' lives are as dangerous and violent as those of their real equivalents and Omri learns the responsibilities of ownership. (9+)

54

VICTORIA WHITEHEAD *The Chimney Witches*, illustrated by Linda North, Orchard Books

This is an excellent witchy story, full of pranks and magic rather than spooks and evil spells. The noises in the chimney keep Ellen awake at night. Determined to find out what is going on, she investigates and discovers Weird Hannah and her unruly son Rufus. Ellen joins them for some midnight adventures with goblins and ghosts before going back to bed. The fantasy elements of *The Chimney Witches* are light and well controlled. (7+)

MISCHIEF
AND MAYHEM

CHAPTER SIX

FUNNY RHYMES, PICTURE BOOKS, songs, stories, jokes or poems – all of these add immeasurably to the strength and success of children's books. There are many and various ways in which books are designed to make children laugh. And they do. Children love funny books. Whenever it is left to them to compile their own list of favourites they come up with the books that have made them laugh.

Humour plays a large part in children's lives. They laugh a lot, they clown about. They have no set rules about what is funny and what is not. Almost anything, especially if it is repeated until the listening adults are driven to distraction, can be uproariously funny. And all the things that make children laugh are in books. They may be verbal or visual. They may be stories which are funny in the telling or the content – or both. The writer's observant eye can detect the funny side of many different situations.

Words alone, even just sounds, can be a source of amusement long before a child has much vocabulary of its own. Babies laugh at the explosive 'POP' in 'Pop Goes the Weasel' or the 'Wee, wee, wee all the way home' in 'This Little Piggy Went to Market'. They love the moment in Eric Carle's *The Very Hungry Caterpillar* when the egg goes 'POP' and out comes a tiny and very hungry caterpillar. They delight in the 'SPLASH' as all the animals · fall into the water in John Burningham's *Mr Gumpy's Outing*. These expressive sounds produce an instinctive reaction. Hearing them leads babies to a delight in wordplay when they come to speak themselves.

A natural inclination in this direction means that when they are older they will be entranced by a collection like Michael Rosen's *Hairy Tales and Nursery Crimes* which contains witty, rhyming poems such as 'Jack and the Tin Stalk', 'The Fried Piper of Hamelin' and 'Goldisocks'. The straightforward juxtaposition of unusual words makes for simple laughter on one level, but the joke is actually a double one which will be fully appreciated and enjoyed by those who already know the originals.

The exhilaratingly inventive language which Roald Dahl employs in The BFG will encourage children to take their own verbal games into new realms. The BFG's continuous and deliberate misuse of language has become a kind of subculture among children who have listened again and again to the story. As in Hairy Tales and Nursery Crimes, the joke is a double one. It uses funny sounds but also very careful wordplay. Maximum pleasure comes from knowing the words that are being played on – helicopter becomes bellypopper, and torpedo, porteedo, and so on. The story encourages children to listen to and look at language in general and to observe the richness and complexity of its structure.

Made-up words, unusual sounds, verbal jokes and wordplay are just one aspect of the many kinds of humour which enrich children's reading. At the picture book level and in illustrations for all age groups, there are all kinds of funny pictures. One of the most skilful executors of children's cartoon illustration (not strip cartoons) is Quentin Blake. His artwork is exceptional in that it is profound in content while remaining easy on the eye. At the first glance you know it is funny, at the second you know why and you know that it is a lot more than just funny. His pictures for the very young in books like Mr Magnolia are sensitively zany. His illustrations to accompany Russell Hoban's complicated weather fantasy, The Rain Door, give exuberant and convincing substance to concepts such as thunder.

In a more tender mood, there are his drawings for John Yeoman's The Hermit and the Bear. The Hermit advertises for a pupil and, after waiting fifteen years, is delighted when the Bear comes along to learn. But teaching the Bear has its problems since he does everything absolutely literally and without any common sense. The eccentric and patient Hermit and the sweet-tempered, innocent Bear are charmingly portrayed in both the gently humorous text and the delicate pictures. Domestic chaos and happiness are shown in his illustrations for Michael Rosen's witty poems in Quick, Let's Get Out of Here! and Don't Put Mustard in the Custard. These books hilariously capture the details of breakfast with burnt toast, the love of an old trainer and much more. There are few things that Quentin Blake has not illustrated and there are no books – even ones on such apparently unfunny subjects as the medical problems raised by children in *Ask Dr Pete* by Peter Rowan – which his comic style has not transformed. He has an exceptional ability to inject amusement into everything and his view of life is always benign.

Raymond Briggs has a less kind eye than Quentin Blake. He uses cartoon strip illustration to give a comic appearance to stories which make sharp and original observations. The best example is his unconventional interpretation of the Father Christmas story in *Father Christmas* and *Father Christmas Goes on Holiday*. His irreverent view of the crusty old gentleman, who uses doubtful language and is shown in such natural and unglamorous situations as on the lavatory, has delighted children, while parents still dispute the propriety of debunking the sacredness of the myth. To be shocked by these details is to miss the point of the whole. The Father Christmas books are funny and delightful because of the way in which Raymond Briggs looks at Father Christmas. The joke is the way Briggs turns him into an ordinary person doing a job which has many disadvantages – including terrible working hours and weather conditions.

Rude or crude humour in children's books is harder for adults to enjoy. The adult is ambivalent about these kinds of jokes. Some find them genuinely unfunny, others feel that children themselves are quite inventive enough in this field without needing books to reinforce a stage which most parents hope will be shortlived. For whatever reason many adults do not enjoy it with the same completeness as children. Yet it plays a large part in many children's lives and it is certainly an area of humour which really makes them laugh.

Where it is well handled, as it is by Raymond Briggs or Roald Dahl, it should be accepted and enjoyed. There is nothing cheap about the way they get their laughs. In *Father Christmas* one frame of Father Christmas on the lavatory is only a tiny part of a much greater whole and if it draws the reader in, at the expense of a little propriety, it has done no harm. Roald Dahl's popularity rests on many claims but humour is certainly an important element in much of his writing. He has never backed away from the rude or crude. His argument is that it makes children laugh and one of his prime intentions is to be funny.

Amidst so much benign good humour, as in *The BFG*, a few jokes about farting and burping should certainly not be disparaged.

Raymond Briggs applies the strip cartoon technique in unconventional ways, whereas in Hergé's Tintin stories both illustration and text keep close to the cartoon conventions of people being zapped and powed, seeing stars and developing large, throbbing swellings. The success of Tintin, the boy detective who has wild and outrageous adventures with his dog Snowy through thirty titles, starting with *The Adventures of Tintin*, lies in the quality of its invention and its meticulous attention to detail. This kind of artwork is obviously funny. It is designed as such and follows certain well-established traditions for making people laugh. But there are plenty of other kinds of picture books which make their jokes in different and sometimes less obvious ways.

From very early on, children see the ways in which pictures can make jokes. They delight in the kind of joke found in Pat Hutchins's *1 Hunter*, a picture counting book in which the reader can see the hidden animals while the hunter cannot because they are behind him. The joke is in the way the book has been designed as much as in the execution of the pictures. A book like this or Anthony Browne's *Bear Hunt* (described in Chapter Two) doesn't proclaim its humour like the more obvious cartoon styles. It is funny for the child who looks at it closely and finds the joke within it. Books like this play an important part in showing children how well rewarded they can be if they look carefully and well.

Just as *Hairy Tales and Nursery Crimes* and the language in *The BFG* are a double joke if the originals are well known, so is Allan and Janet Ahlberg's *The Jolly Postman*. This is a witty book of letters from various fictional characters to each other – Goldilocks's letter of apology to the Three Bears, for instance, and a jolly holiday postcard to Mr V. Bigg, Mile High House, Beanstalk Gardens, from a little boy called Jack. *The Jolly Postman* is a book of exceptional invention. Its clever construction, with envelopes holding the real letters which can be taken out and read, gives the impression of something specially made to be enjoyed by each of its readers.

The laughs in James Stevenson's *There's Nothing To Do!* come from the description of a ludicrous situation illustrated in cartoon pictures: 'Outside, all day long, the cows kept yawning. The birds were so bored, they kept dozing off and falling out of the trees.' So begins Grandpa's story of what happened when he and his little brother were left alone for what looked like a boring day on the farm.

More subtle humour comes in books where the joke is in the pathos of the story – the character and the settings – as in the Stanley Bagshaw books by Ron Wilson. *Stanley Bagshaw and the Fourteen-Foot Wheel* and *Stanley Bagshaw and the Mafeking Square Cheese Robbery*, to name but two, tell of some very narrow escapes that befall the simple-minded Stanley who wears long shorts, glasses and a sleeveless Fair Isle pullover, and lives 'in the North where it's boring and slow'.

Funny picture books are especially important for children who are just beginning to read. The swashbuckling clumsiness of John Ryan's Captain Pugwash stories, such as *Pugwash and the Mutiny* or *Pugwash and the Fancy Dress Party*, the completely zany, rhyming humour of *The Berenstain Bears and the Missing Dinosaur Bone*, by Stan and Jan Berenstain, make a very effective and tempting introduction to reading because children really want to read them.

59

What makes people laugh is perhaps more than anything else a question of taste. Humour can be very obvious and crude or it can be subtle and delicate. When the central situation in a story is inherently absurd the humour is obvious, and children love the ridiculous possibilities it offers. Jeff Brown's *Flat Stanley* is a good example of this.

FLAT STANLEY

When Stanley is squashed by a notice board he remains an ordinary boy – but flat. In this guise he can be flown like a kite and indulge in all sorts of unlikely but easily imagined exploits. Child readers are very amused by his exciting but not always comfortable predicament. Robert Leeson's funny situations in *The Third-Class Genie* come from the wayward magic which Alec's young genie produces. Readers will sympathise with Alec and laugh at the terrible tangles in which he unexpectedly finds himself.

Dick King-Smith's animal stories have brought about a radical reassessment of the genre in the last ten years. As a former farmer, his knowledge and understanding of animals is complete. He uses all this to excellent effect in his writing, and his books are without whimsy or anthropomorphic sentimentality. The animals are firmly based in the farmyard though he takes some licence with their abilities. The results are hilarious and wholly original. In his first book, *The Fox Busters*, he turns farmyard lore on its head when the chickens attack the foxes. More recently in *The Sheep-Pig* he has a runt piglet being brought up by a sheepdog and learning how to herd sheep. The pig is kind and considerate and talks politely and intelligently to the sheep instead of bullying and nipping them as the dogs do. His results are spectacular. The joke is the unlikely – even impossible – idea of a sheep pig, and the humour is accentuated by the understated tone.

Dick King-Smith, Jeff Brown, Robert Leeson and many others invent funny stories. Their books are easy to enjoy and are clearly intended to amuse. Literary satire, on the other hand, makes a joke out of a literary style or convention that already exists. The inverted fairy stories such as Babette Cole's *Princess Smartypants* and *Prince Cinders* in picture books or Jeremy Strong's *The Karate Princess* (for older children) assume knowledge of a story convention and then make fun of it.

Yet another kind of humour comes from authors who write funny books about things that are not intrinsically funny. Diana Wynne Jones's books treat the supernatural, the magical and the mysterious with respect but also with enormous humour, an approach which appeals to those who do not like the deadpan tone of most fantasy. In *Eight Days of Luke*, David is haunted by Luke who appears every time David strikes a match. But David needs Luke to get his own back on the strange and gruesome relatives he lives with. The

mealtime battles between the aunts and grandparents which are judged and awarded points by David, and David's own battle with the housekeeper, make a wonderful setting for this light fantasy. Diana Wynne Jones's observations of people are always penetrating and funny.

Mary Hooper's *Lexie* is the story of two girls staying with their Dad after a divorce and discovering how lonely and helpless he is. Selfishly, the girls wonder how they will survive his terrible cooking and having to do all the chores themselves, but they are also sad to see their Dad in such a mess. Mary Hooper's sharp perception makes this a very funny story. *The Duck Street Gang* could be an ordinary school story but the description of the school Christmas play and the way the girls muscle their way in by insisting on some decent speaking parts is very funny indeed. Denis Marray shows us the ridiculous side of things that happen in every school.

Some ages and stages lend themselves particularly well to humour. The uncontrolled fury of toddlers can be very amusing – especially for those who are not directly involved. Children not much older love to see how they once were and would sometimes still like to be. Teenagers, too, though often treated to nothing but introspection and gloom in fiction, are an easy target. Their mixture of intensity and apparent casualness can be harmlessly mocked. Sue Townsend does exactly that in *The Secret Diary of Adrian Mole Aged 13¾*. Its startling success comes from Sue Townsend's ability to make light of all manner of potentially fraught situations which in real life are usually handled with more worthiness than wit or sense. Her laughter is with her characters rather than at them.

Humour comes into all sorts of books. It cannot be categorised or confined to a type, and it certainly cannot be restricted to specific age groups. Like all responses, the effect of a particular book will depend on the individual. Funny books don't necessarily produce belly laughs. Sometimes their wit is gentler and more personal but, whether visually, verbally, by situation or satire, they entertain as surely as any other medium.

62

FURTHER READING

ALLAN AHLBERG *Woof!*, illustrated by Fritz Wegner, Puffin

When Eric wakes in the night with an itch inside the collar of his pyjama jacket, a tingling in his hands and feet, his nose becoming cold and wet and his ears floppy, he doesn't panic. He just thinks sleepily, 'I'm turning into a dog!' Not everyone would be as cool and calm as Eric when faced with his new doggy life, nor would they be as determined to discover exactly what causes the doggy changes. The how, what and why of Eric's doggy life make up the substance of *Woof!* which is a very funny story, reinforced by strong characters and a plausible school and home setting.   (8+)

HUNTER DAVIES *Flossie Teacake Strikes Back*, illustrated by Laurence Hutchins, Fontana

Flossie Teacake finds being only ten years old distinctly boring. If only she were older she would have much more fun. Then Flossie discovers that she *can* be older. A quick change of clothes, slipping on her sister's fur coat and changing into the sophisticated Floz gives her a chance to sample teaching a ballet class, working in a boutique and standing in for a gypsy fortune teller. Flossie as Floz fulfils many ten-year-olds' fantasies with enormous panache.   (8+)

FLORENCE PARRY HEIDE *The Shrinking of Treehorn*, illustrated by Edward Gorey, Puffin

Boys don't shrink, they only grow taller. But Treehorn is definitely shrinking. He's getting smaller all the time. His father can't stop him, though he tries. Even the teacher who speaks to Treehorn firmly about the impossibility of shrinking in class can't stop the boy from nearly vanishing. Can Treehorn stop himself? *The Shrinking of Treehorn* captures the fun of changing size, the irritation it causes and the different perspective it gives. (8+)

SHEILA LAVELLE *My Best Fiend*, Fontana

Sheila Lavelle's light touch makes this a supremely funny book about the rather awful things that Charlie and her best friend – or fiend – get up to. Charlie follows Angela's lead enthusiastically even though it is she who always gets the blame when the marvellous ideas go disastrously wrong. Anyone with a best friend who sometimes goes a bit too far will know how Charlie and her Mum and Dad feel!

(8+)

ROGER MCGOUGH *The Stowaways*, Puffin

The narrator and his best mate Midge are determined to see life and have adventures. Stowing away seems like a good first step but stowing away on the Mersey Ferry doesn't exactly get you very far. Their other attempts at adventure come to similar ludicrous, unlikely and unlucky ends. Roger McGough has invented some dotty situations and his deadpan writing makes them extra funny. (8+)

63

64

CLASSICS
OLD AND NEW
CHAPTER SEVEN

CUTTING ACROSS ALL the barriers of age, subject-matter and message are the classics. These books are the giants in the field. They have set trends, shaped tastes, set standards and pushed forward our conception of what a picture book or story can be. Some have already lasted through one, two, three or even four generations, and others are books whose current popularity makes them seem likely to last for several generations yet.

There are many kinds of classics and they seem to require many different ingredients. But they all – whether old or new – have some features which make them identifiable. The crux is the author's ability to absorb the child fully in the story. This means going beyond the level of moment to moment entertainment, excitement or pathos. It means enabling children to identify with the story by offering them something which is emotionally timeless, universal and comprehensible. For this, an absolute understanding of a child's perspective is essential. Some authors gain this understanding from their experience of children either as parents or professionals. Teachers, for example, are well placed to observe them accurately and to commit those observations to their stories. But there are many children's illustrators and writers who claim not to know children well and certainly many who have never had children of their own. Instead, their empathy comes from memories of their own childhoods. They can recreate the things that are common to all about being a child because they hold them powerfully within their own minds.

If a deep understanding of childhood is the primary key to the making of a classic, another factor is the author's ability to offer the reader a contained and complete world. Not a complete world as in a fantasy world, since many classics are set firmly in the real world and the present time, but a world in which the characters, the place and the action are convincing enough to stand on their own. As a reader you enter the world of that particular book and become involved in its binding inner structure which shuts out everything else.

It is not just children who are held by stories of this kind, even though they have long been classified as 'children's books'. Indeed, many of the great so-called children's classics, such as Lewis Carroll's *Alice's Adventures in Wonderland* or J. M. Barrie's *Peter Pan* and even, to a lesser extent, Kenneth Grahame's *The Wind in the Willows* are enjoyed considerably more by adults than by children, who sometimes find the humour and content difficult. Most children's classics appeal to both adults and children. The complete understanding of the child's view and the creation of the enclosed world will affect adults just as strongly, if not as directly. Occasionally there are books which appeal almost equally to adults and children. The recent outstanding success of *The Secret Diary of Adrian Mole Aged 13¾* (described in Chapter Six) lies in the fact that Sue Townsend's very funny book offers much for both teenage readers identifying with themselves and parents who are trying to 'understand' them.

All the following books and many of the books mentioned in other chapters have one or other – or both – of these qualities. Their obvious differences in subject, style and plot show that the classics need not be a restricted or rarefied diet. They are the books which should not be missed in a lifetime of reading; the ones to be passed down from one generation to another to form an important shared literary heritage.

Beatrix Potter's animal stories (*The Tale of Peter Rabbit*, *The Tale of Mrs Tiggywinkle* and *The Tale of Jemima Puddle-Duck* are perhaps the best known) have immediate appeal because of their sheer physical charm. The quality and accuracy of Beatrix Potter's beautiful watercolours convey tiny details of the world the animals live in, while the child-scale format makes them easily accessible to young readers. Far beyond this, she combines real animals with their human counterparts to create a new and lasting animal world. Her animals are convincing as animals but also respond like humans, so giving two levels of enjoyment. None of her stories shy away from the harsh realities of animal life – Peter Rabbit's father was, after all, 'put in a pie by Mrs McGregor' – but they also show animals being capable of rational thought, speech and the rest. In *The Tale of Jemima Puddle-Duck*, for instance, both Jemima and the Foxy gentleman are entirely animal in their habits and instincts but have the trappings of human behaviour.

For the same age group, and equally absorbing but with a quite different setting, are Edward Ardizzone's Little Tim books. These stories capture young listeners' imaginations by letting them share Tim's obsession with the sea. From *Little Tim and the Brave Sea Captain* on through the many stories about Tim and his friends Charlotte and Ginger, the child listener can identify fully with the young boy whose passion for the sea leads him to adventures of one kind or another. Of course most of them would, in reality, be entirely impossible. That is the charm. Edward Ardizzone's sympathetic but witty illustrations can stand a great deal of scrutiny.

67

Of a more recent vintage is John Burningham's *Mr Gumpy's Outing*. This has a simple and entirely satisfactory build-up as more and more animals pile into the boat until its eventual, splashy conclusion. Children will be delighted by the predictability of each animal doing the one thing it has expressly been asked not to do, and the cool and witty illustrations match the text perfectly.

There are numerous books whose special qualities have ensured their survival; stories which children, now grown up, remember with such affection that they want *their* children to know and love them too. There is a particular pleasure to be had from sharing your own favourite book with your child. A. A. Milne wrote *Winnie-the-Pooh* and its sequels for his son, whose nursery animals it features. The stories, which bring Pooh bear and his friends to life, have an enchanted quality which survives from one age to another because of the integrity of the character of each animal and their interaction together. Pooh, Piglet, Tigger, Eeyore, Kanga and the rest entertain all children when they hear about them. Reading *Winnie-the-Pooh* aloud shows just how much this is a book passed from parent to child.

For a slightly older audience but still on the subject of a much-loved toy having a life of its own, is Ursula Moray Williams's *The Adventures of the Little Wooden Horse*. Full of pathos but not sentimentality, it tells the story of the beautiful, hand-made wooden horse that nobody buys from the old wood carver. Instead, the horse sets out to earn its own living and suffers all kinds of terrible experiences in so doing. Some children love this kind of tragic story. They identify fully with the poor sad horse, suffer with him when times are bad and are genuinely elated when the going gets good again. They cry but they enjoy it too. For others this kind of sorrow is just too much to bear. You have to judge your own child. Levels of empathy vary enormously.

The same emotions flow through E. B. White's *Charlotte's Web*. Charlotte the spider heroine, Templeton the rat and Fern the farmer's daughter are all determined to save Wilbur the pig. It is Charlotte's clever plan and brilliant execution of it that has the real impact but the cost is Charlotte's life. I defy any child, even one who really *hates* spiders, to remain unmoved by this story. Fern, Charlotte, Templeton and Wilbur's own determination to change the adults' minds invites the reader to put his all into willing them to succeed. It is a book which revolves around child and animal power. Though more humorous than *The Adventures of the Little Wooden Horse*, its sadness is sharper and even harder to bear.

The world of *The Borrowers* is neither a real one nor a ghostly one but something in between, which is just as absorbing and magical. Pod, Homily and their daughter Arrietty live under the floor in a big old house. Their home is reached through a hole in the wainscot under the clock on the landing. Mary Norton describes their tiny home in absolute detail. It is entirely furnished by all those things which disappear so mysteriously from our own houses. The real delight of the book is this kind of detail and the picture it gives of these small-scale people who borrow everything, including their names! Their adventures keep the story alive but the events in the narrative are not the essence of the book. In sequels the Borrowers go Aloft, Afloat and Afield but the magic of the enclosed world is then lost in a welter of action.

A whole world of a quite different kind is captured by Laura Ingalls Wilder in *Little House in the Big Woods*. This is the first in a series of books about Laura and her family as they move further and further West into the new territories being opened up across America. In the Big Woods there are bears, heavy snows and a wonderful family Christmas as well as wholly absorbing insights into the daily life – and especially the food – of a pioneering family of that time. Laura Ingalls Wilder is telling her own life story through these books and we see all the experiences through the eyes of the little girl that she then was.

LITTLE HOUSE IN THE BIG WOODS

Laura's very deep love for her Pa comes through strongly so that we, too, come to know this strong, affectionate man who let his daughter be as liberated as was possible in those days. Because this is so much a book of memories it has an intimacy which speaks very directly to its readers and makes them at once at home with the Ingalls family and their way of life.

For those who like to get stuck into this kind of series where the enclosed world is extended through many books, *The Children of Green Knowe* by Lucy Boston is the first in an almost equally large number of related titles. This and all the others revolve around Green Knowe – a house with an immense history. Present-day children and the Oldknowe children from generations back become easy friends in this delightful ghost story. Lucy Boston has created a magical world here and those who enter it become as absorbed as she is in the minute detail of this very special old house. Children who are themselves affected by place and atmosphere will understand the point of the Green Knowe books and be touched by them.

Penelope Lively's 'haunting' in *The Ghost of Thomas Kempe* is a far lighter and funnier affair than that of the Green Knowe books but it carries some of the same intense feeling of how directly the past and present can be brought together by a particular place. In the carefully controlled time slip Thomas Kempe, a seventeenth-century sorcerer who has been walled up for hundreds of years, seizes the arrival of James and his family in the old house as an opportunity to get a new apprentice. Lots of misunderstandings and strange happenings make this a very funny book which almost disguises how much it says about the role of the past in so many things that occur in the present day.

Tom's Midnight Garden is also a book of atmosphere and, although its plot revolves around contact with a past world, it has none of the thrilling or chilling aspects associated with traditional ghost stories. Instead it is a novel of exceptional depth which looks closely at the sense of lost identity from which we all sometimes suffer. At the centre of the story is Tom who, unhappy and sleepless, discovers a magical hour of happiness in the dead of night. Philippa Pearce's understanding of a lonely and unhappy child is total, and her carefully constructed resolution in the midnight garden provides excitement as well as emotional satisfaction.

A special garden makes a private world of a very different kind in Frances Hodgson Burnett's *The Secret Garden*. Mary and Colin, both lonely and unhappy children, find strength in their friendship when they meet in this secret and neglected place. In a world without adults, or only distant ones, Mary changes herself from a spoilt, bad-tempered little girl into a strong and determined one. She then sets out to change Colin too. Perhaps more than any other book, *The Secret Garden* combines a totally child-centred story with encapsulation in a private, encircling world. The result is a book which offers magic to many children.

Much less fanciful but equally child-centred is *Carrie's War* by Nina Bawden. Like Mary in *The Secret Garden*, Carrie is in an unfamiliar environment. She is sent with her brother to Wales – as a war evacuee. The book has drama in it but its greatest strength lies in Carrie's understanding of the difficult domestic situation in which she and her brother find themselves.

In *Thunder and Lightnings* the friendship between two boys, dull Victor and newcomer Andrew, develops because they are both outsiders. Victor allows Andrew to share his passion for the Lightnings that fly overhead and gradually life changes for both. Jan Mark is always deeply perceptive and makes her points gently. Andrew and Victor wrap themselves up in the aeroplanes and so protect themselves from the knowledge of their isolation from the other children.

Both *Carrie's War* and *Thunder and Lightnings* are very much domestic dramas. In the first, the situation of being an evacuee plays a part in the absorbing nature of the story but it is the totally child's-eye view that gives it a lasting and special quality. In the second, there are very few dramatic props but Jan Mark's ability to write about friendship in a voice that children can believe and from a viewpoint with which they can identify – these are what make it a book of such strength.

71

CARRIE'S WAR

It is not the weight of time that makes books classics. These last two, both written in the last twenty years, show that it is the way the author holds the child's attention and takes them into the world of the story that makes them great. They also prove that new books add to old traditions. As parents, sharing favourite books with one's children is always a treat but should not preclude moving on to the best books of a new generation.

But do children themselves choose the same 'best books' or are their criteria completely different? Why are the books which children adore so often despised and abhorred by adults? The qualities which are the essence of classics apply to all books chosen by children themselves, whether they are 'approved of' by adults or not. Their prime feature, as far as the children are concerned, is that they are totally engrossing. The difference lies in what can only be defined as literary quality. Particularly where children's reading is concerned, adults have a narrow-minded attitude to quality which makes them believe that the goodness of a book must lie in its literary and educative excellence and not in its sheer readability.

Both positions have right on their side. The best classics are highly readable and without doubt there is something extra to be gained from reading books of literary excellence. On the other hand, a child who is reading a book should not be discouraged just because it is not a literary book. If in the pursuit of excellence you kill the enjoyment of reading then you have done harm.

Roald Dahl's books lie at an interesting halfway point in all of this. He has written novels of stature such as *The BFG* (described in Chapter Six) and the highly original fantasy odyssey *James and the Giant Peach*. His storytelling gift is exceptional and he is massively inventive. He is also very much a 'writer'. He creates powerful private worlds and his stories are completely child-centred. He is adored by children and yet makes many adults uneasy. Whether it is because of his delight in the rude, crude and slightly nasty, or whether it is because his books are so readable and therefore look like a soft option, is hard to define.

For me, he is an author (like many others) whose books need to be considered individually. He can be cruel and crude. He intends to be – knowing that children have that within them. He can also be revolting, as in *The Twits*, in a way that few adults but many children find appealing. But he can be very tender too, as he is in *Danny, the Champion of the World* – a story which describes a very special father and son relationship with simple affection. Much of his writing has the same sort of purpose as fairy tales. It does not *make* children have nasty thoughts, it gives them a framework in which to indulge them.

Sometimes full of stereotypes, sometimes surprisingly penetrating about how individuals react, Roald Dahl should not be dismissed just because he is so popular. Unlike many of the other writers whose books are top choices for children his books speak strongly. He is not repetitive in plot or character, he offers constant surprise – even shock. He is neither trivial nor mundane.

Roald Dahl is at a halfway point because his books are both classic and dubious, and also because his individual books vary so much. Most selection by children favours the author rather than a particular book. Indeed, one of the most appealing features for children is the mass of a writer's work. While adults may shudder at the repetitiveness of the plots and characters of particular authors it is just this quality which makes children enjoy them. There lies safety and security and familiarity, something that is of great importance to children who are only just becoming confident readers.

And so, bearing in mind that as an adult one will not have to pass too much time with these authors, it is worth trying to understand why children like them so much. Enid Blyton is the author that adults love to hate. It is easy to say that her books are predictable and full of stereotyped characters. The writing is pedestrian and the vocabulary limited. But many children adore them. Though best known, perhaps, for her Noddy books, her most valuable contribution is in the area of easy-to-read fiction. The numerous adventures of the Secret Seven and the Famous Five – *Five Get Into Trouble* and *Five Go To Smuggler's Top*, to name but two – are loved by children because they are exciting but safe, and if you can read one you know that you will be able to read the next and the next and the next.

73

For an older age group, Judy Blume's books are similarly popular because of their 'sameness'. In addition, they have the advantage of being about the kind of problems which obsess pre-teenagers for a brief but intense spell. *Blubber* speaks to the child who worries about being overweight. *It's Not the End of the World* explores the anxieties which children experience when their parents divorce. They indulge – possibly even foster – many hang-ups which we would rather our teenagers *didn't* have. But they speak to their audience in a vocabulary and tone which they can easily understand and enjoy.

Rupert Bear, the Mr Men, the Chalet School stories, even the lovable but predictable Postman Pat whose every story starts with a description of the extraordinary weather conditions in Greendale – these success stories need never be specially selected for children. They will be discovered without adult intervention. If they are enjoyed they need not be weeded out. Since they lack the appeal for all ages which marks out the greatest classics they will be part of a stage that is passed through. As such, they contribute to keeping children 'hooked' on books. They are part of a reading heritage while making no claims to being classics of style, plot or character.

FURTHER READING

RUSSELL HOBAN *The Mouse and His Child*, illustrated by Lillian Hoban, Puffin

When the key in his back is wound up, the mouse father can dance and lift his little child high into the air. Joined by the hands they dance and dance until the motor runs down and they are still. This is the mouse and his child. The story follows the toy from its good start as a much-treasured toy in a careful family, through its consignment to the scrap heap and the domination of the cruel Manny Rat, until its final journey to a happy home. From the first moment when a tramp covets the delightful mouse and his child through the window of a toy shop, Russell Hoban gives lasting life to the fantasy of the toy and its adventures. (9+)

ERICH KÄSTNER *Emil and the Detectives*, Puffin

Travelling alone on a train to visit his grandparents, Emil is robbed of the money he had pinned so safely inside his jacket. He is determined to get it back but, instead of calling the police, he joins forces with a gang of children who chase the thief and retrieve the money. The ultimate in gang stories, *Emil and the Detectives* is also an exciting and credible adventure. (9+)

MICHELLE MAGORIAN *Goodnight Mister Tom*, Puffin

Goodnight Mister Tom is a rich book, stuffed full of sentiment and emotion. Thin little Willie is evacuated to the country at the outbreak of the war. He is billeted on Tom Oakley, a crusty widower who has shut himself off from the village since the death of his young wife over forty years earlier. Willie has been beaten, frightened and neglected all his life. He arrives stitched into his underclothes and with a belt in the parcel packed by his mother 'for when he's bad'. (The story of his life may be too harrowing for some.) Lonely Tom comes to life again with this small boy to love, while Willie grows physically and mentally stronger in his tender care. And then there is Zach, the strange evacuee whose friendship does so much for Willie; the other village

74

children, learning to read and write and, above all, discovering his ability to draw. Filled with drama, unhappiness and happiness, *Goodnight Mister Tom* is a hard book to put down.   (10+)

E. NESBIT *The Railway Children*, Puffin

When their father is wrongly imprisoned, family life is radically changed. The three children and their mother move to the country and a quite different way of life. Left on their own a great deal, Roberta, Phyllis and Peter explore their new surroundings and particularly enjoy the train which runs through a cutting at the bottom of their garden. They make friends with the stationmaster and devise a campaign to ensure that their father's case is properly brought to trial. E. Nesbit's children are as resourceful and independent as contemporary children might be and their adventures still make excellent reading.   (10+)

75

ANNA SEWELL *Black Beauty*, Puffin

One of the most passionate animal stories of all, *Black Beauty* is the story of a horse told retrospectively by himself. It was deliberately written 'to induce kindness, sympathy and an understanding treatment of horses'. It triumphs because the animal's view is convincingly 'horsey' while also being full of insights into contemporary society and so of interest to more than just horse lovers. *Black Beauty* is a long book but its simple first-person – or animal – narrative makes it easy to read.   (10+)

76

FAIRY STORIES
AND FOLK STORIES
CHAPTER EIGHT

MYTHS, LEGENDS AND fairy tales are the stories that children should really *know*. Familiarity with the best fairy stories and the key myths and legends is the surest foundation for all subsequent reading. They are for all ages, classes, cultures, creeds and for both sexes. They can be read aloud or alone and they can even be used, in a simple form, for learning to read. They can be read and re-read in different versions. They are funny, sad, frightening, mysterious and magical. They are the original stories from which so many other stories have evolved.

Across cultures, myths and legends have certain unifying features. They have survived because they are good stories but also because they contain vital and lasting truths. They revolve around loyalty, honour and courage. In British mythology the Arthurian legends certainly contain these principles, as do the stories of Theseus from Greek mythology, the Rama and Sita stories from India, and many more. These stories also make judgements about good and bad. They may not be the same as our own judgements but they have a powerful internal logic and provide a strong sense of right and wrong.

By contemporary standards, some of them are unnecessarily brutal and cruel but then in the societies in which they were originally set, violence was a far more accepted part of everyday life than it is today. We still live in a society with too much violence in it but we have made rules about what is allowed and what is not. Killing has been outlawed except in official times of war. Fairy stories, in particular, are often criticised for their violence and apparent delight in it. The retribution that the wicked stepmother receives in 'Snow White' from Virginia Haviland and Raymond Briggs's *The Fairy Tale Treasury* is certainly nasty: 'For they had ready red-hot iron shoes, in which she had to dance until she fell down dead.' Examples like this are easy to find in fairy stories from all sources.

Should children be encouraged to think that this kind of punishment is acceptable? Should they be frightened by stories such as 'Little Red Riding Hood', which brings violence right into the loving relationship with a grandmother? Will they not be given nightmares by giants such as the one in 'Mollie Whuppie', who wants to kill the little girls, or witches as in 'Hansel and Gretel', or stepmothers like Cinderella's, or wolves, or fire-breathing dragons or any of the other monstrous characters who play central roles in fairy stories? The psychologists' answer fits well with most parents' experience. Children do have violent thoughts (as do adults) but they are not going to be made violent by reading stories of this kind. Instead, these stories are going to give them a framework in which it is safe to have such thoughts. In this make-believe world they can live out their wildest and most aggressive fantasies. The stories give free rein to many of the thoughts that children have but cannot express themselves, and they can gain understanding through the vicarious experience.

There may also be a particular benefit in this kind of story for modern children. Death features much in fairy stories. People die and others grieve. Often they grieve wildly and violently. Children who live in an age where death is hardly mentioned, and grieving is largely a private affair, are particularly in need of this kind of vicarious experience. Folk and fairy stories also display all sorts of other emotions just as powerfully. The cruel side is tempered by love and loyalty. These are tested in the stories just as they are tested by children in real life. Underlying the story of the frog prince is the idea that love must be proved in adversity as well as under favourable conditions.

Envy is a very basic human emotion and one that recurs in fairy stories. On a one-to-one level there is hope for all younger siblings in the stories of those youngest sons who share their humble crusts with misshapen characters in forests and are rewarded while their older brothers are punished. There is a sense of fairness in fairy stories which children appreciate. It appeals to their own sense of justice.

Children well understand the emotional logic of fairy stories. They love the rags-to-riches convention and the idea that the lowest can become the greatest. They, too, are small and weak but aspire to and dream of better things. We have all felt ourselves to be

Cinderellas in one way or another at certain times. On a less personal scale, the convention of the rich suitor being defeated and the poor but honest boy rewarded is of equal importance. The juxtaposition of the 'haves' and 'have nots' is as relevant today as it was when these stories were first written. The message that material wealth is no guarantee of happiness needs to be reinforced in an age of overwhelming materialism. The fairy tale formula with castles, fabulous jewels, gold and all its trappings set against the poor woodcutters, farmers, cottagers and widows makes its points far more tellingly and subtly than most modern stories of the same kind.

All fairy and folk stories follow particular conventions. In the majority, male and female roles are deeply stereotyped, with the girls playing largely passive parts while the action revolves around the men. However, on closer examination, there are some traditional fairy stories where the girls play significant and heroic parts. Mollie Whuppie is one such. She defeats the horrible giant entirely by her own wit. Even princesses can sometimes do more than spin, and their stubborn refusal to marry the prince of their father's choice often gives them control over their own destiny.

In *The Woman in the Moon*, James Riordan looks at some of the powerful heroines from folk and fairy stories who have been forgotten and passed over in favour of their more passive sisters (like Cinderella and the Sleeping Beauty). The stories in this book tell of Gulnara the Tartar Warrior, Lone Bird and Caterina the Wise, who have slipped into obscurity. Their stories show them to be courageous and resourceful, providing excellent positive contrasts to the traditional image. Stories such as these are in the minority but it is well worth seeking them out so that the impression left by fairy tales is not hopelessly one-sided and chauvinistic.

Recently there has been a determined attempt to give princesses a stronger and more positive role in fiction, in books such as Martin Waddell's *The Tough Princess*, where the princess refuses to marry the ninny who is chosen for her and sets out to find a husband for herself. These kinds of stories turn the stereotypes on their heads in a most satisfactory way.

Folk stories are not necessarily any crueller than fairy stories but their world is less glossy – the characters do not usually drip with jewels or sparkle with gold, or have good fairies who can bring about

79

THE WOMAN IN THE

magical changes. They are at least partly 'real'. Many of the values and central themes are similar but at the heart of the folk stories there may be a kernel of truth. The myths of King Arthur, for example, have grown out of the true stories of an unusually powerful king.

This central character is one of the big pulls of folk and fairy stories. Children love stories where the characters have more skills or powers than other mortals. Myths and fairy stories, with their blend of reality and something larger than reality – magical powers, god-given strengths or god-given protection – provide a tradition which has been copied throughout the ages. It still flourishes today with larger-than-life characters like Superman, He-man or the Thundercats. Like their literary forebears, these characters have some human characteristics (usually stereotyped ones) as well as extra-human powers which come from a variety of sources, some magical and, nowadays, some technological.

81

The strong central character gives readers a chance to embark on a controlled fantasy in which they can assume a pivotal role and, in so doing, be completely involved. The story of the young Arthur who pulls the strange sword from the anvil, when much older men have failed, is exactly the stuff of childhood dreams. It is the beginning of the stories about King Arthur and his knights of the round table which make up the core of Celtic mythology. From that point on, his story has the blend of fact and fantasy – reality and magic – found in all the great myths and legends. These wonderful stories of King Arthur and his knights have been retold in numerous versions. Rosemary Sutcliff's *The Sword at Sunset* is sophisticated, romantic and atmospheric. Roger Lancelyn Green's *King Arthur and his Knights of the Round Table* is a much simpler and more 'factual' account, while T. H. White's *The Once and Future King* is whimsically inventive, making it especially suitable for older readers.

Stories from Greek mythology have played a large part in the entertainment and education of British children and therefore British writers. The stories are magnificent and many have at their centre larger-than-life figures such as Theseus, Jason and Hercules, who are portrayed with a similar blend of fact and embellishment. Perhaps because of the decline of Greek and Latin in schools, there are few recent retellings of these classical stories and hardly any for the very young, who would enjoy the action of the myths even if they could not appreciate their finer points. Michael Gibson's *Gods, Men and Monsters from the Greek Myths* is clear and easy to read with bold illustrations to match the text. It lacks lyricism but it tells the stories plainly and makes a sound introduction.

For older readers the most comprehensive retellings which give a sense of the originals – both in action and atmosphere – are Roger Lancelyn Green's *Tales of the Greek Heroes* and *The Luck of Troy*, both of which are highly readable and stuffed full of action. There is also *The Faber Book of Greek Legends* by Kathleen Lines, which is more atmospheric but less dramatic. Anyone who was brought up on the Greek myths will always remember the stories and characters. They contain heroes and heroines whose actions stick in the mind. Icarus who flew too near the sun, the cunning of Theseus and his escape from the Minotaur, or the drama of Jason and the Argonauts – all these stories should be sought out and *not* forgotten by future generations.

But not all myths and fairy stories are about strength or even about good versus evil. Myths are also necessary to describe or to help us understand the very basis of our existence. Traditionally, for British children, a central core of these stories came from the Bible. With the less central position of religion in society and education, the original versions of these stories are being lost. Instead they are being adapted to different media. In the Middle Ages the stories were illustrated by stained glass windows; today they are the basis for plays, operas and musicals such as *Joseph and his Amazing Technicolor Dreamcoat* or *Noye's Fludde*. Their success in these new forms reflects their outstanding qualities which make them such suitable and powerful material for almost any form of entertainment.

The decline in children's knowledge of Bible stories is compensated for by the attention that is now given to the mythologies of other cultures. The richness of Indian mythology is fully conveyed in *Seasons of Splendour* by Madhur Jaffrey. The stories are magnificent and the intelligent structuring of them, so that they follow the course of the Hindu year, gives the collection a particularly powerful internal logic.

Stories from the Caribbean do not have a religious base but the importance of the animal world and its interaction with mankind is an essential part of West Indian and Afro-American culture. James Berry's collection, *Anancy Spiderman*, tells the tales of Anancy and the magic and trickery which enable him to be king of the animals even though he is so small and weak, while the Brer Rabbit stories, which were adapted in the United States after they had been taken there by the black slaves, show a similar emphasis on trickery and cunning.

From other cultures the myths are only available piecemeal. *When the Night Came* by Joanna Troughton is a beautiful retelling of an Amazonian myth about the coming of the night. In Australia the Aborigines' Dreamtime stories are set in a time when the land and the animals in it were taking shape. They are their creation stories, and show how the physical conditions of a country play a considerable part in determining different creation myths.

It is a mark of the continuing relevance of these stories that they survive translation, abbreviation and adaptation but remain vivid and telling even in different cultures and times. They have been passed down through many centuries and generations, offering both entertainment and insight into times past and other cultures. As sheer entertainment they have a quality which sets them apart from many contemporary stories. As sources of information about the world around us, and about the essential human truths and how they have been interpreted by other people at other times, they are beyond compare.

83

FURTHER READING

JUDY CORBALIS *The Wrestling Princess and Other Stories*, illustrated by Helen Craig, Knight

Judy Corbalis turns the conventional princess roles inside out in these stories which give new life to the fairy tale tradition. The princess in the title not only wrestles but also drives a fork-lift truck. Her plans for getting a husband are certainly original and make a witty contrast to the usual fairy tales with kings, princesses and princes all playing their set parts. The other stories in the collection poke gentle fun at conventional role-playing. This is non-sexism at its lightest.

(6+)

AXE-AGE, WOLF-AGE

KEVIN CROSSLEY-HOLLAND (RETELLER) *Axe-Age, Wolf-Age*, illustrated by Hannah Firmin, Faber

The dangerous, violent and mysterious Viking past is exposed in this atmospheric collection of some of the greatest Norse myths. As traders, raiders and conquerors, the Vikings needed suitably warlike gods. But, as ordinary people, they also needed an explanation of the universe, of how the world and the people on it came to be. Starting with 'The Creation', the myths in this collection show us a Norse view of the world which reflects their own way of life. The striking language and strong characters make the stories particularly powerful. (9+)

GRACE HALLWORTH *Mouth Open, Story Jump Out*, illustrated by Art Derry, Magnet

The night-time is the Devil's time when anything sinister or unexpected might happen. Grace Hallworth's collection of stories is set down from the oral stories told in Trinidad and Tobago. The unnerving blend of real and supernatural gives all the stories a tingling, spine-chilling quality which is powerful enough to leave even the most hardened sceptics little room for doubt. Grace Hallworth manages to capture the distinct nuances of the spoken originals, giving the book a very special flavour.   (8+)

TERRY JONES *Fairy Tales*, illustrated by Michael Foreman, Puffin

Terry Jones has adapted the traditional fairy tale and made it his own. This is a collection of thirty original and inventive stories which combine the essential fairy tale ingredients of magic and morality. There are dragons and witches, fear and happiness. These fairy tales, though not classic, are so well constructed that they fit the classic tradition perfectly. They are especially good for reading aloud.   (4+)

NAOMI LEWIS (RETELLER) *Stories From the Arabian Nights*, illustrated by Anton Pieck, Methuen

This is a collection of thirty from the one thousand and one tales known as 'The Arabian Nights' which Shahrazad told the king in order to stay her day of execution. They are magical, mysterious and extraordinary stories which capture the imagination, just as they held the king spellbound night after night. They are closer to fairy stories than mythology even though they come from a specific culture and reflect certain aspects of it. 'The Magic Tale of the Ebony Horse', 'The Tale of Ala Al-Din and the Wonderful Lamp' and, perhaps most famous of all, 'The Tale of Ali Baba and the Forty Thieves' – all of these and more are given life in Naomi Lewis's retellings.   (7+)

86

TEENAGE READING
CHAPTER NINE

READING, THAT VITAL SKILL which children spend so much time acquiring somewhere between the ages of five and eight, is often almost totally abandoned only a few years later. Is this the fault of the books or the readers? Neither, of course. There are several possible reasons for the fact that teenagers, in general, don't read much. Lack of time, lack of interest, the absence of a suitable image – all of these contribute to making teenagers less than committed readers. In order to hold their attention, the theory is that fiction must be created especially for them. It must be on their terms. The subject-matter, the idiom, the language, the mores must be right on. Books must be cool, trendy, OK. To this end the need for 'teenage books' as a special genre has long been recognised and authors and publishers have produced books accordingly.

The theory has some truth in it, but there is also a high risk of being patronising. To assume that teenagers are only interested in romance, sex and the angst of growing up is belittling. The commitment shown to Live Aid, anti-nuclear demonstrations and fundraising for all sorts of medical and social charities shows other teenage preoccupations which also need to be reflected and explored in fiction.

In other words, teenage readers, just like younger readers and adult readers, need a variety of fictions. They are not a separate *kind* of being; they are just at a different stage. In fact, books for older readers or teenage fiction – call it what you will – is not absolutely cut off from the rest of fiction, either younger or older. It is not read exclusively by teenagers, nor are they the only ones who read it. Most so-called teenage books will be lapped up by precocious readers long before the actual teens are reached. Equally, many teenagers will be reading adult books alongside the books directed specifically at them.

But because the teens are a time for developing independently and finding things out for yourself, teenage fiction must explore the same areas. Should it direct society or follow it? Are teenagers corrupted by what they read or reassured? It has been interesting to watch the changes in what is and is not considered acceptable. When *Forever* by Judy Blume was first published in this country in 1976 it caused an uproar. Explicit sex between teenagers in a teenagers' book was thought to be potentially dangerous. It was part of a wave of books, many from Sweden, which made teenage sex the norm. I don't think anyone actually knew if it was. Part of it seemed to be adult pressure. Adult writers wanted to show their new-found liberation which may well not have been shared by the next generation.

In reaction to it came books like Ursula Le Guin's *A Very Long Way from Anywhere Else* which describes the relationship between two cool, cerebral teenagers, both of whom find it hard to cope with the sexual expectations pushed on to them by the media and parents, but who enjoy a happy friendship. In *My Darling, My Hamburger* Paul Zindel makes his points about teenage relationships in a story which revolves around two couples who are treating being 'a couple' in quite different ways. The book offers choices. Zindel is understanding and compassionate and shows that he knows something of how it feels to be an adolescent.

Currently the trend is much more in this direction. Even before AIDS, teenage books had backed away from explicit sex, or even any sex, in favour of love, loyalty and friendship. Margaret Mahy's *The Catalogue of the Universe* is the best recent example of this. She captures the ease which Tycho and Angela, who are long-standing friends, have with each other. There is an underlying sexuality but it is clearly secondary to the emotional support they give one another.

But new areas of controversy are being explored. Jean Ure's teenager in *The Other Side of the Fence* is at odds with his parents because he tries to explain to them that he is gay. Jean Ure has written a sympathetic novel in which she promotes tolerance and understanding. She is not pushing her readers into being gay but she is exposing and discussing something that has not been much covered in teenage reading. Intelligent, thought-provoking books about teenage relationships are an extremely important antidote to the traditional romances (such as 'Sweet Valley High') which are invariably chauvinist and stereotyped. Even so, no one should be brought up on an unadulterated diet of romance – whether sexual or 'just good friends'. As I have said, there is much more to teenagers than that and much more to the fiction written for them.

There are the powerfully directed books that put specific issues before readers who want to think, and there are books which are just excellent stories without having any particular message to drive home. Among the first, the problems of racism, for example, are tackled in a variety of ways and in different settings. *Sumitra's Story* by Rukshana Smith is written in the first person and tells of the confusing double life in which many Indian girls living in Britain are trapped.

89

The full horrors of apartheid in South Africa are exposed and explored in Toeckey Jones's *Skindeep*. Rhonda is white, with all the trimmings that wealth can buy, in a society where servants – slaves, almost – are an accepted part of life. She falls in love with the strange new boy at school. Dave is kind, caring and intelligent. Their relationship develops but there is an underlying tension. And then, on a visit to Cape Town, the truth comes out. Dave comes from a poor black family. His unusually pale skin has allowed him to be classified as a 'pass white'. But that is not enough. The relationship has been illegal. It comes as a shock to find that even relationships can be governed by law.

For many years Marjorie Darke has been writing books whose storylines revolve round a political struggle or campaign. In *A Question of Courage* she gives a vivid account of a young girl's involvement in the suffrage movement. Her description of the force-feeding of those on hunger strike is all too memorable. In *The First of Midnight* she tackles the abolition of slavery in Britain, while *A Long Way to Go* tells of the anguish which faced conscientious objectors to conscription in the First World War and their special kind of bravery. In each of her books she shows how individuals have stood up for good and important causes. The rights and wrongs of their struggles now seem obvious but the courage it took to stand firm against a society in which these things were not so evident is powerfully conveyed.

The men and women who helped the slaves in America to safety in Canada needed a special kind of bravery too. Based on the true story of the underground railroad, *Underground to Canada* by Barbara C. Smucker follows the successful but nerve-wracking escape of two young girl slaves. On a more contemporary note, *A Game of Soldiers* by Jan Needle is a very chilling antidote to any romantic notions that teenagers might have retained about the Falklands War. Seen through the eyes of Sarah, Thomas and Michael, three children who, like most children, think of war as a glorified game, it shows the stark, violent and brutish side of any war.

James Watson's *Talking in Whispers* is a bit less brutal and a lot more sinister. Andes is only sixteen but he is a wanted man. He is wanted by the secret service for his part in the struggle against the Junta. His life is in danger but he and his friends are determined to go on fighting for their ideals. *Talking in Whispers* shows the extreme danger faced by anyone working for the resistance movement in Chile more powerfully and more directly than any number of news bulletins. The impact of books like *A Game of Soldiers* and *Talking in Whispers* is enormous. Teenagers badly need good books on these important subjects to help them learn and judge the bad – and good – things in the world around them.

Fears of a nuclear disaster have led to many post-bomb novels and books about anti-nuclear protest. Robert Swindells's *Brother in the Land* retains some positive feeling despite its depressing subject and its all too realistic look at how people would conduct themselves in such circumstances. Louise Lawrence goes further into the future in *Children of the Dust* and describes an alarmingly mutated race. Joan Lingard's *The Guilty Party* is less apocalyptic. Instead, she looks at the conflicting loyalties of a committed anti-nuclear protestor and shows that it is almost as difficult to flout consensus opinion now as it was for the suffragettes or conscientious objectors in Marjorie Darke's novels.

Issues of all kinds can make good fiction but you do not need an issue to make a good book. Since the 1960s there have been a great many outstanding writers for teenagers. Many have not written contemporary or topical books but their understanding of people and their responses has been assured. Issues, opinions and settings may vary but human attributes remain unchanged, which is why old stories don't die even though they may go out of fashion.

Books of this kind also last because of the sheer quality of their writing and the way they provoke intelligent thinking. It is patronising to assume that teenagers will only be kept reading by soft, 'easy', sloppy writing. Under the slick airbrush covers, it is vital that the writing is of the highest quality, whatever the subject. It is this which will ultimately make the book worthwhile. In this category come writers such as Jill Paton Walsh, whose *Goldengrove* and its sequel *Unleaving* give teenagers a chance to read an adolescent-centred story written in a wholly adult style, or Leon Garfield, whose *Smith* reveals a squalid, eighteenth-century London full of mystery, suspense and fear. Jane Gardam's books, *Bilgewater* and *The Summer After the Funeral*, are elliptic novels which reflect a highly perceptive teenager's view of life. Adèle Geras's *Voyage* is an intense story set on board a boat full of immigrants bound for a new and more prosperous life in America. The conditions are hard and the travellers, though strangers at first, are dependent on one another for survival. The human interaction set against the physical deprivation on board is utterly absorbing.

91

Jan Mark has written fiction of many kinds. Her writing is always witty and her subject-matter original. Her stories can be very light, as in *Frankie's Hat*, a collection of three short stories, each of which gives a tantalising glimpse of a different kind of teenager. Or they can be more substantial, though equally invigorating, as in *Handles*. Here, Jan Mark tells the story of Erica, whose passion is hanging round the multi-storey car park with a motorbike gang, and how she survives summer in the depths of the country. Like Jan Mark, Peter Dickinson

HANDLES

is a writer whose sheer originality of subject-matter and ability to write so many kinds of books make him stand out. *Tulku* is a fast-moving adventure story with a most unusual, Tibetan setting and a strong, resourceful central character.

Janni Howker's career as a writer is still new but she has already made a significant contribution with *Badger on the Barge*, an emotionally probing collection of short stories which looks at friendships between different generations, and with her two novels, *The Nature of the Beast* and *Isaac Campion*. Paula Fox is another author who is always deeply perceptive. She shows a genuine and profound interest in what her characters think and why. Her themes and characters range widely but they are always convincing and absorbing. In *The Moonlight Man* she tackles the feelings of a sixteen-year-old who spends a summer with her father whom she has always idolised but never known.

All these writers provoke thought through their narratives. Some go even further by offering something more disturbing, something actively nasty, which needs to be considered carefully. Robert Westall challenges the reader in many of his books. He does so most strongly in *The Scarecrows*, a tremendously powerful and thoroughly nasty book about a boy's passionate hatred of his new stepfather. Simon's venom, guilt and terror are almost tangible and the psychological explanations ring true. The story can be dismissed on the grounds of taste (there are certainly some very tasteless moments in it) but it is a book which demands a response and, sadly perhaps, it is a book which some children will find valuable in their own struggle to come to terms with their families and themselves.

Robert Cormier's writing is always provocative and his books touch on the harsher side of reality with startling intensity. In *The Chocolate War* he describes the violence behind a protection racket that is officially organised within a Catholic school. *The Bumblebee Flies Anyway* is a fascinating and yet sinister book in which Cormier forces readers to consider boundaries between sanity and insanity.

These many and diverse titles show convincingly that just because children are younger than adults they do not need to be addressed at a lower literary level. Books like these do not have a particularly strong teenage idiom but they make very effective reading. Teenage interests are reflected in readable fiction because it is well written as much as topical. And now it is even being properly packaged. Teenagers have recently been identified as a group with strong purchasing power. Since then books have been directed expressly at them. They are published as paperbacks with suitably attractive covers. Gone is the dowdy 'bookish' image. Instead, the aim is to make teenagers feel good with books. The fact that books are still sold in bookshops, and not among records or clothes, retards the complete breakdown of barriers but at least books are now in with a chance. The horse has been taken to the water. There is every reason for it to drink.

FURTHER READING

All these books are suitable for readers of 11+.

PETER CARTER *Bury the Dead*, Fontana

Set against a background which probes the social differences between East and West, *Bury the Dead* looks sharply at the insecurity of present comfort in a world where the past may still reveal unpleasant secrets. The Nordens are comfortably placed in East Berlin. The parents have good jobs and satisfactory enough accommodation. Grandmother lives with them, maintaining the best traditions from her previous Prussian life while also revelling in the triumphs of fifteen-year-old Erika. Erika is an outstanding high-jumper with a chance of a glamorous life as an international competitor. Then Uncle Karl arrives. Where has he been and what has he been doing? He is rich and successful. In his wake come the police and from then on life for the Nordens is changed for ever. *Bury the Dead* is a thought-provoking and disturbing book.

ROSEMARY HARRIS *Zed*, Magnet

Zed is a taut and compassionate thriller. Thomas is held hostage for four days. For the four long days of the siege he is shut up with the others in a small room. He sees cowardice, courage, cruelty and unexpected kindness, and at the end he emerges as a far more likeable and understanding person. Rosemary Harris captures the terror and the relief, the anger and the sympathy with equal success.

JOAN LINGARD *The Twelfth Day of July*, Puffin

Against the background of the build-up to the huge Protestant celebrations on 12th July, Kevin and Sadie become friends. Their different religions make it risky for them even to meet, but they are determined to break away from the traditional prejudice that governs majority thinking in Belfast. Joan Lingard shows how life goes on even under such conditions and how a pair of teenagers react against this kind of repression. *The Twelfth Day of July* is the first in a series of books about Kevin and Sadie, all of which are a highly successful combination of romance, politics and religion.

JEAN MACGIBBON *Hal*, Puffin

Long before he knows her real name, Barry knows Hal and gives her the nickname 'The Indian Queen'. From his window he watches Hal and her friends playing on the derelict site after school. Hal doesn't know Barry, or even that he is there, until the day that he is able to warn her of danger. From then on a friendship develops between the two lonely but very different children. Jean MacGibbon shows how varied childhood can be and how important peers are at this stage.

K. M. PEYTON *Flambards*, Puffin

For sheer romance, drama, hatred and excitement there are not many stories that can beat *Flambards*. The first in a quartet of titles, it describes a young girl's arrival and subsequent life as part of a family which revolves around horses, dogs and drink. Christina has never met her cousins Will and Mark, or her uncle, but she soon discovers that each has a steely determination and that Flambards is a cheerless house. She finds her escape by falling in love with Will, while he escapes through dreams of early flying machines.

BOOKS AS
SOCIAL COMMENT

CHAPTER TEN

NLIKE OTHER MEDIA which give out information when *they* want to, books are available whenever the child wants them. Children read for narrative but they also read for information. They read factual information on how to groom a pony or the workings of the planets, but they also read information of a more general kind. And this kind of reading develops their attitudes towards society. Even the simplest of stories, and picture books especially, have an underlying message. The behaviour of the characters, the situations in which they find themselves, the choices they make – all these give particular, though often subliminal, messages to the readers.

95

Throughout the last decade and before, authors, illustrators and publishers have become increasingly aware of the need to reflect the changing patterns of British society. The very marked sexual stereotyping in children's books was badly in need of re-examination. For years Mums in pictures and stories wore skirts, washed up, cooked and worried. They rarely drove cars and certainly wouldn't have known how to mend one. Some of these characteristics still apply to some women but certainly not to all. Dads, too, needed a new image. They needed to be seen as carers rather than merely financial providers.

Recognition of this has led to radical questioning of sexual stereotypes. Anthony Browne's *Piggybook* makes a joke out of the lazy chauvinist father and his lazy chauvinist sons whose features become increasingly porcine as their behaviour deteriorates. But under the joke lies a deadly serious message. The mother leaves home because her family is so demanding, and only returns when they accept their share of the housework and leave her free to do what she most enjoys

PIGGYBOOK

96

– mending the car. No one is saying that all homes are, or should be, run like this. The point is for books to recognise an alternative to the traditional division of labour between males and females.

More extreme role-changing is shown in *Through My Window* by Tony Bradman and Eileen Browne. Here, the Dad stays at home to look after the little girl while Mum is out at work. Again, this will not be the norm for everyone but it is a family pattern which is common enough and should therefore be portrayed in books. After all it is important that children living in this situation should also experience the reassurance of finding their own lifestyle reflected in the books they read.

It is not only the role of women that has changed. Family structures have become far more flexible – or far more complex – and this, too, is expressed in fiction. *Are We Nearly There?* by Louis Baum and Paddy Bouma describes a poignant, and yet not exactly sad, journey for father and child, as they return to the child's home with his mother after spending a weekend together. Mothers on their own now feature prominently and positively. The Mums in these books are confident and capable, like Alex's Mum in Mary Dickinson's *Alex's Bed*, who just gets on with whatever needs doing – making Alex's new bunks, for instance.

This is not to say that the problems of changing family circumstances are ignored. There are a great many books, especially for teenagers, which deal with unhappiness of one kind or another – worries about money, the sadness of the parent left behind or the loss of security for the child. But it is now acknowledged that there are many families which are not Mum, Dad and two smiling children, and they are given a positive and confident image in fiction.

These books are entertaining but they are also didactic. They deliberately set out to affect how children think – not that there is anything new in this. Traditionally, literature for children has always contained moral messages. The earliest books were for improvement and instruction, usually only lightly disguised as stories. Later the story became more important but the message remained. *The Little Princess* by Frances Hodgson Burnett is a wonderful and piteous story about a little girl who lives a life of luxury until her parents die, leaving her penniless and dependent on her own resourcefulness, but it is also a homily on the importance of goodness and the transience of wealth.

It is only in this century that the idea of reading wholly for enjoyment has become so widely accepted. And even today it is impossible for books to be entirely message-free. This is inevitable for two reasons; partly because, consciously or subconsciously, all authors have opinions which pervade their books, and partly because children are so easily influenced. They are a susceptible audience. Their own experience is limited, which means that their responses to the new experiences which make up so much of their reading are not their own but those of the writer.

The attitudes conveyed in books therefore have an enormous influence, especially on very young children, and this is why the changing images in picture books are so important. It is to be hoped that today's children, as a result of growing up with picture books showing less rigid family patterns or of reading fiction with a wider view of life, will be more tolerant and open-minded about all social issues.

In the near half-century since the Second World War, the population of Britain has changed substantially. Children's books of the post-war period largely reflected the attitudes of the comfortable, traditional, white middle class. The majority of writers came from that section of society themselves. This does not mean that they were

97

prejudiced or conservative, or that their values were wrong, but their fiction showed only a small slice of society then and an even smaller slice of society as it is now.

The changes in family patterns have become widely accepted in books. At the same time there has been a powerful move to make fiction more representative of all classes and cultures. Increasingly, writers, publishers and readers are becoming aware of the need to give all children positive images of themselves and each other. Errol Lloyd's *My Brother Sean* and *Sean's Red Bike* are good domestic picture book stories about a black family. In *The Conker as Hard as a Diamond*, Chris Powling's hero Alpesh becomes the conker champion of the universe. Both these books are naturally multicultural. The message is at the heart of the book and there is no overt point to make.

98

The problems of a child who arrives in this country without any knowledge of the language or customs are thoughtfully portrayed by Geraldine Kaye in *The Beautiful Take-Away Palace*. Kai Cheng knows no English and is bewildered and isolated at school until he is befriended by Amy. Many children will have been silent observers of such a situation in their own classes. This story, and others like it, carry an active message which will make it easier for children to understand and help in a similar situation.

Jan Needle tackles the problems of racism head-on in *My Mate Shofiq*. The violence and hatred which prejudice can cause are set against a friendship between two children who ignore the possible serious consequences, and concentrate instead on their own relationship which they are determined will survive. Farrukh Dhondy writes about teenagers – black and white – in *Come to Mecca*, a collection of short stories which encourage tolerance while also making a clear case for black identity. Delivering the same message in a slightly different way are books which show a different culture in its own right. Virginia Hamilton's difficult but powerful *A Little Love* describes black American life. The terror of two black teenagers when they cross the stateline into Tennessee is tangible and truly scary. In forcing recognition of the horrors of racism, *A Little Love* should act as a powerful deterrent to any racist thoughts. Anita Desai's *The Village by the Sea* sets the absolute poverty of village life against the corruption of life in Bombay and, in so doing, gives her readers an understanding of some aspects of Indian life and values.

Folk stories, fairy stories and the mythologies of other cultures and religions also play a huge part in increasing children's knowledge, and therefore tolerance, of worlds beyond their own. But this tolerance should not be gained either by lowering standards of writing or by distorting society. There are cases where the search for tolerance has gone beyond what might be defined as sensible positive discrimination, where authors and publishers have scrambled to show their liberal idealism. It is therefore vital to maintain the quality of writing in order to avoid the trap of providing moral tracts, as in earlier times, rather than enlightening fiction.

Specific information about some of the things that have traditionally set children apart or made them feel different, like physical or mental handicap, is also available in books and plays a part in making our society more tolerant and understanding. Books alone cannot solve the problem but they can be an effective way for children to externalise their own fears. Anxieties are reduced if they have enough knowledge to comprehend the issues, instead of building up frightening and often inaccurate fantasies.

Most importantly, books which concentrate on a specific issue may encourage parents and children to discuss it. Sharing a book which reflects an actively or potentially worrying situation can be easier than confronting the problem outright. Once the first barrier has been broken down it may be much easier to face the real situation. Hiding emotions is very confusing for young children. They do not have the experience to cope with most problems on their own.

The book as therapist can seem a long way from the enjoyable story but, if skilfully handled, the two may be successfully combined. Althea Braithwaithe was at the forefront of this kind of publishing in its early days. When her own marriage split up, she found that there were no books which were at all appropriate for children as young as her son Duncan. None of them looked at the straightforward practicalities of seeing both Mum and Dad but in different places, and none of them explored the reasons why parents might split up. There were no books aimed at reassuring children that the break-up of their parents' marriage was not their fault. Althea wrote a book on this subject herself and since then she has written and published many more on other problematic subjects. She looks at death in *When Uncle Bob Died*, the first day at school in *Starting School* and in *Going into Hospi-*

99

tal the feelings of children going to hospital. Her books have been extremely successful for well over a decade. As she says, 'They help adults and children to talk. Often it is adults who find it difficult to share their emotions and a book can help. For the children these books are often just good stories which can be appreciated as much as any other picture book.' Thus, her books work on two levels – as entertainment and, if so required, as a useful source of information and a focal point for discussion. They are all cheap paperbacks directed specifically at parents.

Today there are an enormous number of books dealing with every likely – and unlikely – subject under the sun. Starting school, visiting the dentist, having an operation, the birth of a new baby, getting glasses – all these subjects are aired in picture book form, some with illustrations and some with photographs. Nigel Snell's Problem Solvers series includes titles such as *Danny is Afraid of the Dark* and *Sally Moves House*.

100

Recently there has been a spate of books which warn children about sexual abuse. Orale Wachter's *No More Secrets For Me* is a collection of four short stories which are scary because of their implications rather than because they are overtly violent. In each one a child is frightened by an adult who invades his or her natural privacy. *Gillyflower* by Ellen Howard is a deeply sad story of a little girl who is persistently abused by her father. She feels guilty and unclean which makes her unable to make friends. She also dreads the possibility of the same thing happening to her much-loved younger sister. Clearly, these books need to be used with the greatest of care, which means being shared with a child, not just left about for the child to pick up on their own. Professionals working with children who have been abused claim that these books can play an important role in relieving anxiety, though many adults find them depressing and potentially frightening.

Talking to children about books that discuss social issues reveals something about how they perceive them. Andrew, a five-year-old with glasses, told me, 'I liked *Johnny Gets Some Glasses* because I was scared my friends would laugh when I first got mine. I wanted them to read the book too so that they would know how I felt.' This stands in sharp contrast to the oft-quoted adult perception that 'children know something terrible is going to happen to them when they are given a "problem" book!'

That books shape attitudes is undeniable. The messages they put over, whether as fiction, 'faction' or straightforward fact, will influence children. Whether they should reflect society as it is or impose a view of society as it could, or should be, is a matter of opinion. And whether books that do not reflect our ideal vision of society should be banned is also a matter of opinion. What is important is that the written word is a powerful tool and a potential force for social change, for reassurance and for education. All books, not just those in this chapter, have that potential within them.

FURTHER READING

CLARE CHERRINGTON *Sunshine Island, Moonshine Baby*, illustrated by Jennifer Northway, Fontana

This collection of stories from the West Indies is told to a little girl as she unwillingly sits in on her grandmother's sewing sessions. Each of the old ladies tells a story from her own childhood on the different islands that make up the whole group. Some are funny, some sad, but each is lyrical in its own way and together they add up to a magical collection. They also give an insight into the way of life in the West Indies in the recent past when current grandparents or even parents were growing up.

(6+)

BABETTE COLE *Princess Smartypants*, Fontana

Babette Cole's witty and vigorous artwork shows how alternative a princess can be. Princess Smartypants likes to be Ms. She has no intention of getting married to a wimpy prince. Determined to weed out the duds, she sets her suitors a series of Herculean tasks. The traditional princess story is nicely inverted in this picture book for younger readers.

(9+)

ROSA GUY *The Friends*, Puffin

Edith and Phyllisia are both outsiders. Newly arrived in Harlem from the West Indies, Phyllisia is disliked because she is quick and clever and speaks with a different accent. Edith is also an outsider but for different reasons. She gets to school late and always looks a mess. At first, Phyllisia is wary of Edith's friendship but when she really does need help she sees what good friends they can be. Rosa Guy empathises with these two outsiders and shows how much they are both strengthened by friendship. (11+)

HADLEY IRWIN *A Girl Like Abby*, Puffin

At first glance, *A Girl Like Abby* looks like a typical teenage novel. Chip admires the cool, self-contained, attractive Abby but he can't seem to get close to her. There is a mysterious barrier around her. And then Chip discovers the reason. Abby is the victim of incest. It seems impossible. Her father is a respected member of the community. They are a happy, caring family. But it is true, and Chip has to help Abby get the help which she so desperately needs. Hadley Irwin handles the subject with delicacy and sympathy. (12+)

JILL KREMENTZ *How it Feels when Parents Divorce*, Gollancz

This is a collection of nineteen first-hand accounts of how children from seven to seventeen felt when their parents divorced. The details of each case are different but the emotions, the confusion, the anger, guilt, sorrow and the acute sense of loss are all very much the same. Some have more or less come to terms with it, others remain resentful and sad. Though a depressing book in some ways, reading about other children's experiences may be useful for children who are going through the same thing. (9+)

POETRY

CHAPTER ELEVEN

Poetry is poetry
It may be good
It may be bad
It may be happy
It may be sad . . .

Some like poetry
Some detest it
Some write it beautifully
By now you must have guessed it.

It may rhyme
Like this
And may be sublime
Like this
It may make sense
It may not
It may make pounds, shillings and pence
It may not.
A poet must have a good imagination
Like Shakespeare
He should have satisfaction from his creation.   PETER (AGED 9)

THIS IS AS full and tidy a description of poetry as you could wish for. Poetry is an inventive and flexible way of communicating which has always carried with it the risk of being treated as a specialist and rather difficult literary form. In fact poetry is a form of writing which is especially suited to children. Like Peter, many children take an instinctive delight in poetry. They like it because it is rhythmic, jingling and short. These qualities make it more approachable than a stretch of continuous prose.

The rhythmic delight begins in babyhood. From then on, the nursery rhymes and lullabies discussed in Chapter 1 are among the first speech patterns, apart from ordinary conversation, that a child will hear. And they are poetry. Even without being conscious of it, children begin to appreciate poetry.

Their early delight in rhythm and careful word use is evident. 'Humpty Dumpty sat on a wall/Humpty Dumpty had a great fall' has a simple beat which helps the young listener to understand the words. The fall is down; the beat is down. Alternatively, 'Hey, diddle, diddle, the cat and the fiddle/The cow jumped over the moon/The little dog laughed to see such fun and the dish ran away with the spoon' has a fluency which gives charming credibility to the idea of a dish running away with a spoon. Listening to this kind of verse delights babies and gives them a taste for rhythmic descriptions long before they may be ready to absorb poetic concepts or emotions.

But for many children poetry stops with nursery rhymes. A good poetry anthology should be used alongside a collection of nursery rhymes and from then onwards, all through childhood. *The Young Puffin Book of Verse*, edited by Barbara Ireson, is an upbeat, cheery collection of poems with lots of illustrations. The careful selection of young poems makes this an excellent first anthology while also proving convincingly that poetry is for everyone. For older and more sophisticated readers and listeners, *The Rattle Bag*, edited by Seamus Heaney and Ted Hughes, is a comprehensive choice of much of the best British and American poetry for children. It is laid out alphabetically by title which makes it especially free from whimsy or contrived classification.

For funny poems, Roger McGough's *The Kingfisher Book of Comic Verse* is a mighty selection of over 200 humorous poems, old and new. Poems of all kinds in one book are the surest way of introducing children to many different poets. This will give them a chance to sample, test and decide which kinds of poetry they like especially.

Collections of a single poet's work may not give so much choice but they will certainly offer a rich selection of poems for all moods and occasions. There is a particular pleasure and satisfaction to be had from the different voices and styles of a single poet. Seeing a whole range of poems often gives a surprisingly different view of a poet than can be conveyed by the few much-anthologised, best-known ones.

Individually, the poems of Edward Lear are widely known, with 'The Jumblies' as many children's favourite, but a whole collection increases their impact and shows the astonishing range of his invention. Holbrook Jackson's collection, *The Complete Nonsense of Edward Lear*, with wonderful, spidery illustrations by Edward Lear himself, does this perfectly. Michael Rosen's *Quick, Let's Get Out of Here!* is a book of enormous vigour which is appreciated equally by four-year-olds and ten-year-olds. *Early in the Morning* is a collection of forty of Charles Causley's fresh, nursery rhymes which capture the feel of traditional verse while adding something new of their own.

Whether in single poet collections or mixed anthologies, poetry is perfect for reading aloud. It is short, immediate and bears much repetition. It is also memorable so that it lasts, even if only in fragments, long after the reading is over. Very simple verses, like A. A. Milne's 'When I was One,/I had just begun', are often lisped by children as young as two or three, while slightly older children can often surprise by reciting whole verses of poems which have really caught their fancy.

Most adults can still remember the poems they heard when young – a poem like Walter de la Mare's 'The Listeners' tells a spooky story, the spirit of which is immediately evoked by the opening lines:

> 'Is there anybody there?' said the Traveller
>   Knocking on the moonlit door;
> And his horse in the silence champed the grasses
>   Of the forest's ferny floor.

The passion behind William Blake's 'The Tyger' makes the opening lines unforgettable – even if not understood and often misquoted (or otherwise abused!):

> Tyger! Tyger! burning bright
> In the forests of the night,
> What immortal hand or eye
> Could frame thy fearful symmetry?

Poems that rhyme are the easiest to remember – and the easiest to define as poetry – but they are only one kind of verse. Modern children's poetry has changed dramatically from the scaled-down model of traditional adult poetry which it once was. It has now taken off in directions of its own. It has no set form, no rules about subjects and yet it is still recognisable as poetry.

Without the framework of metre or verse, poetry is less sharply separated from story. The difference lies in a way of using words. Poems often make their points elliptically rather than directly. They use words in particular combinations which evoke mood or scene or character rather than spelling out details and filling in backgrounds. Just by being concise they offer fresh ways of looking at things. This briefest of epigrams by Ogden Nash shows how effective this can be:

> The cow is of the bovine ilk,
> One end is moo, the other milk.

In narrative verse, poetry and story move closer together, though poetic form is still as important as content. In 'The Night Mail', for instance, W. H. Auden uses the rhythm of the poem to recreate the rhythm of the train as it dashes through the night:

> This is the night mail crossing the border
> Bringing the cheque and the postal order
> Letters for the rich, letters for the poor
> The shop at the corner and the girl next door.

Rudyard Kipling does much the same in 'A Smuggler's Song', in which the beat of the horse's hooves sets the beat for the poem:

> If you wake at midnight and hear a horse's feet,
> Don't go drawing back the blind, or looking in the street,
> Them that asks no questions isn't told a lie.
> Watch the wall, my darling, while the Gentlemen go by!

Narrative poems are particularly accessible because they are stories and, therefore, not so obviously 'poetic'. Despite the popular misconception that poetry is 'airy fairy', both the subject-matter and the style of 'The Night Mail' and 'A Smuggler's Song' are plain and straightforward. They tell a story using poetry for what it adds, not just to be fanciful.

Contemporary narrative poems similarly use the poetic form, though not always rhyme or rhythm. Their subject-matter is even more down to earth, which means that they have moved poetry very much into the realm of everyday communication, far from the charges of elitist or rarefied expression. Gareth Owen's 'Street Cricket' from *Salford Road*, for example, brings to life a summer's evening in any urban street:

On August evenings by the lamppost
When the days are long and light
The lads come out for cricket
And play until it's night.
They bat and bowl and field and shout
And someone shouts 'HOWZAT!'
But you can't give Peter Batty out
Or he'll take away his bat.

Probably more than anyone else, Michael Rosen has perfected – even invented – a form of domestic poetry. He writes poetry about the most unlikely subjects – chocolate cake, washing up, even changing a baby's nappy in 'Eddie and the Nappy' from *Quick, Let's Get Out of Here!*:

Eddie hates having his nappy done.
So I say all cheery,
'Time for your nappy, Eddie,'
and he says, all sad,
'No nappeee.'
And I say, 'Yes, nappy.'
So I have to run after him going,
nappy nappy nappy nappy . . .

QUICK, LET'S GET OUT OF HERE!

This kind of poetry speaks very directly to children. All these examples, whether contemporary or not, show that written communication can be as forceful and engaging as speech. There is no mystique or difficulty about reading it; no special subject which makes it poetry. It is funny, easy to listen to, and telling. When poetry is more obviously 'constructed' it may be harder to read but there is still no need for it to be obscure or difficult. The very careful and sparing use of words means that each has to be read and understood. Poetry like this is not for skimming.

In 'Zebra Crossing' Roger McGough gives us his highly original way of looking at something familiar in daily life – not a 'poetic' subject at all. He is both penetrating and witty, and his observations on a zebra crossing will affect how we look at them ever after:

> There is a Lollipopman
> At the zebra crossing
> With lollipops
> He is trying
> To lure zebras across
> He makes me cross.
> I cross.

Where the subject is more obviously poetic, the success of the poem still depends on the poet's original way of looking at it. Robert Frost's 'Stopping by Woods on a Snowy Evening' is a perfectly conventional subject for poetry but Frost gives the reader atmosphere as well as detail. This is much more than a description of a snowy evening:

> Whose woods these are I think I know.
> His house is in the village, though
> He will not see me stopping here
> To watch his woods fill up with snow.
>
> My little horse must think it queer
> To stop without a farmhouse near
> Between the woods and frozen lake
> The darkest evening of the year.

The ability to convey atmosphere intensely in such a brief space is another of the special qualities of poetry. The way the words are put together can tell you instantly whether this is a sad, happy, serious or funny poem. Without the need for elaborate scene-setting you can feel the coldness of the snow in 'Stopping by Woods on a Snowy Evening'. At the opposite end of the scale, showing how light and silly a poem can be, while still conveying a mood, is Brian Patten's 'Squeezes':

> We love to squeeze bananas
> We love to squeeze ripe plums,
> And when they are feeling sad
> We love to squeeze our mums.

All these poems show something of what makes poetry such a special and different way of communicating, while also proving that it is particularly suitable for children – right from the beginning. Poetry should never be set on a pedestal and seen as difficult or inaccessible. Once there is no mystification and poetry is accepted as a special but wholly available form of communication then poems of all kinds can be shared and enjoyed. Their brevity makes them especially suitable for children who want to absorb a message without the concentration needed to listen to a book. Their rhythm and inner logic make them memorable. The combination means that when children are offered the right poetry they enjoy it, and remember it too.

10

FURTHER READING

T. S. ELIOT *Old Possum's Book of Practical Cats*, illustrated by Nicholas Bentley, Faber

'Growltiger', 'Macavity the Mystery Cat', 'The Rum Tug Tugger' – many of T. S. Eliot's cats and the poems about them are known individually. Collected together, their variety and originality are shown off to great effect. They are a superb group of poems which are straightforwardly amusing while also revealing every aspect of every imaginable kind of cat.   (8+)

WALTER DE LA MARE *Peacock Pie: A Book of Rhymes*, illustrated by Edward Ardizzone, Faber

Walter de la Mare's poetry is delightful. Much anthologised, it is also worth having in a collection, to show the range of his poems. His light, gentle touch and sure rhyme are in everything he writes. He is funny, as in 'Miss T.' ('It's a very odd thing, As odd as can be, That whatever Miss T. eats Turns into Miss T.') and sad, as in 'Tired Tim', but mostly his poems are cheerful, easy reading.   (7+)

NAOMI LEWIS (COMPILER) *Messages: A Book of Poems*, Faber

This is a sophisticated anthology for older readers who are already committed to poetry. Naomi Lewis's understanding of the special qualities of poetry has guided her choice of poems not written especially for children, but certainly enjoyed by them. She includes poems by Shakespeare, Shelley, Browning and Wordsworth, as well as by some of the best contemporary and near-contemporary poets, like Stevie Smith, Ted Hughes and Charles Causley.   (12+)

ROGER MCGOUGH *Sky in the Pie*, illustrated by Satoshi Kitamura, Puffin

Collected together in one volume, the full impact of Roger McGough's poetry is properly felt. His poems may be zany, as in the title poem, or funny and self-deprecating, as in 'The Poet Inspired' or 'The Poet Takes a Walk in the Country', but there is always an underlying serious edge which makes them so telling.   (9+)

KAYE WEBB (EDITOR) *I Like This Poem*, Puffin

I Like This Poem shows just how broad a spectrum of poems children enjoy. Selected by children themselves, it includes every kind of poem and poet, from the most traditional to the most contemporary. Because it is a collection of favourites, each chosen by an individual child, it has a particularly enthusiastic feel to it. Most of the favourites are also excellent poems so it stands as a good, comprehensive anthology of some of the best, mostly British, poetry.   (7+)

110

Appendices

111

Booklist

READING ALOUD
CHAPTER ONE

112

Berenstain, Stan and Jan, *The Big Honey Hunt*, Collins

Briggs, Raymond, *Mother Goose Treasury*, Puffin

Briggs, Raymond, and Haviland, Virginia, *The Fairy TaleTreasury*, Puffin

Corrin, Sara and Stephen, *Stories for Five-Year-Olds*; *Stories for Six-Year-Olds*, Puffin

Dicks, Terrance, *T. R. Bear Goes to School*, Piccadilly

Edwards, Dorothy, *My Naughty Little Sister*, Magnet

Elkin, Judith (editor), *The New Golden Land Anthology*, Puffin

Falkner, J. Meade, *Moonfleet*, Puffin

Garner, Alan, *Tom Fobble's Day*, Fontana

Godden, Rumer, *Miss Happiness and Miss Flower*, Puffin

Hughes, Ted, *The Iron Man*, Faber

Kipling, Rudyard, *Just So Stories*, Viking Kestrel

Murphy, Jill, *The Worst Witch*, Puffin

Pooley, Sarah, *A Day of Rhymes*, Bodley Head

Storr, Catherine, *Clever Polly and the Stupid Wolf*, Puffin

Strugnall, Anne, *The Julian Stories*, Fontana

Tolkien, J. R. R., *The Hobbit*, Allen and Unwin

PICTURE BOOKS
CHAPTER TWO

Aardema, Verna, and Vidal, Beatriz, *Bringing the Rain to Kapiti Plain*, Macmillan

Ahlberg, Janet and Allan, *The Baby's Catalogue*, Puffin

Briggs, Raymond, and Vipont, Elfrida, *The Elephant and the Bad Baby*, Puffin

Browne, Anthony, and McAfee, Annalena, *The Visitors Who Came to Stay*, Hamish Hamilton

Browne, Anthony, *Bear Hunt*, Magnet

Burningham, John, *Time to get out of the bath, Shirley*, Fontana

Carle, Eric, *The Very Hungry Caterpillar*, Puffin

Cole, Babette, *The Trouble With Mum*, Fontana

Dupasquier, Philippe, and Waddell, Martin, *Going West*, Puffin

Garland, Sarah, *Going Shopping*, Puffin

Hedderwick, Mairi, *Katie Morag*

Delivers the Mail; *Katie Morag
and the Two Grandmothers*,
Puffin
Hill, Eric, *Where's Spot?*, Puffin
Hughes, Shirley, *Alfie's Feet*,
Fontana
Jessell, Camilla, *Baby's Days*; *Baby's
Toys*, Methuen
Lloyd, Errol, *Nini at the Carnival*,
Puffin
Oxenbury, Helen, *Helping*; *Family*,
Walker
Pragoff, Fiona, *Alphabet*; *Growing*,
Gollancz
Sendak, Maurice, *Where the Wild
Things Are*, Puffin
Varley, Susan, and Willis, Jean,
Monster Bed, Fontana

BECOMING A READER

CHAPTER THREE

Ahlberg, Allan, and McNaughton,
Colin, *Me and My Friend*,
Walker
Benchley, Nathaniel, *Red Fox and
his Canoe*, Puffin
Berenstain, Stan and Jan, *The Big
Honey Hunt*; *Bears on Holiday*,
Collins
Choroa, Kay, *Oink and Pearl*, Puffin
Gage, Wilson, *The Crow and Mrs
Gaddy*; *Mrs Gaddy and the Fast-
Growing Vine*, Bodley Head
Ginsburg, Mirra, and Tafuri, Nancy,
Across the Stream, Puffin
Huddy, Delia, *The Chicken Pox
Party*, Hamish Hamilton
Hughes, Ted, *The Iron Man*, Faber
Lobel, Arnold, *Frog and Toad*,
Puffin
Marshall, James, *Four On the Shore*,
A. & C. Black
Rockwell, Anne, *Cars*, Puffin

Schwartz, Alvin, and Zimmer, Dirk,
*In a Dark, Dark Room and other
Scary Stories*, Heinemann
Seuss, Dr, *The Cat in the Hat*; *One
Fish, Two Fish*, Collins
Smith, Alexander McCall, *The
Perfect Hamburger*, Puffin
Sutton, Eve, and Dodd, Lynley, *My
Cat Likes to Hide in Boxes*, Puffin

ACTION AND ADVENTURE

CHAPTER FOUR

Aiken, Joan, *The Wolves of
Willoughby Chase*, Puffin
Ashley, Bernard, *Taller than Before*,
Orchard
Atterton, Julian, *The Shape-
Changer*; *The Tournament of
Fortune*, Julia MacRae
Avery, Gillian, *The Warden's Niece*,
Bodley Head
Bagnold, Enid, *National Velvet*,
Puffin
Bawden, Nina, *Rebel on the Rock*,
Puffin
Buckeridge, Anthony, *Jennings Goes
to School*, Macmillan
Byars, Betsy, *The Eighteenth
Emergency*, Puffin
Cleary, Beverly, *Ramona the Pest*,
Puffin
Coolidge, Susan, *What Katy Did*,
Puffin
Fine, Anne, *Madame Doubtfire*,
Hamish Hamilton
Forest, Antonia, *Autumn Term*,
Puffin
Golding, William, *The Lord of the
Flies*, Penguin
Kemp, Gene, *The Turbulent Term of
Tyke Tiler*, Puffin
Leeson, Robert, *Grange Hill Rules,
OK?*, Fontana

113

McBratney, Sam, *Colvin and the Snake Basket*, Magnet

Mayne, William, *A Swarm in May*, Goodchild

Paterson, Katherine, *Bridge to Terabithia*, Puffin

Pearce, Philippa, *The Battle of Bubble and Squeak*, Puffin

Pullman, Philip, *The Ruby in the Smoke*, Puffin

Ransome, Arthur, *Swallows and Amazons*, Puffin

Smith, Dodie, *One Hundred and One Dalmatians*, Puffin

Smith, Joan, *We Three Kings from Pepper Street Prime*, Julia MacRae

Sutcliff, Rosemary, *Warrior Scarlet*, Puffin

Swindells, Robert, *The Serpent's Tooth*, Hamish Hamilton

Trease, Geoffrey, *Bows Against the Barons*, Hodder; *Tomorrow is a Stranger*, Heinemann

Treece, Henry, *Viking's Dawn*, Puffin

Voight, Cynthia, *Homecoming*, Fontana

Watson, James, *Where Nobody Sees*, Gollancz

Duncan, Lois, *The Eyes of Karen Connors*, Hamish Hamilton

Farmer, Penelope, *Charlotte Sometimes*, Puffin

Fisk, Nicholas, *A Rag, a Bone and a Hank of Hair*, Puffin

Hill, Douglas, *Exiles of ColSec*, Puffin

Hughes, Monica, *The Keeper of the Isis Light*, Magnet

Klein, Robin, *Halfway Across the Galaxy*, Puffin

Lavelle, Sheila, *The Apple Pie Alien*, Orchard

Le Guin, Ursula, *The Wizard of Earthsea; The Tombs of Atuan; The Farthest Shore*, Puffin

Lewis, C. S., *The Lion, the Witch and the Wardrobe*, Puffin

Mahy, Margaret, *The Changeover*, Magnet

Nimmo, Jenny, *Emlyn's Moon*, Methuan

Orwell, George, *1984*, Penguin

Pearce, Philippa, *A Dog So Small*, Puffin

Sefton, Catherine, *The Blue Misty Monsters*, Faber

Tolkien, J. R. R., 'The Lord of the Rings Trilogy', Allen and Unwin

114

MAGIC AND MYSTICISM
CHAPTER FIVE

Alcock, Vivien, *The Haunting of Cassie Palmer*, Fontana

Burningham, John, *John Patrick Norman McHennessy – The Boy who was Always Late*, Cape

Christopher, John, *The White Mountains*, Puffin

Cooper, Susan, 'The Dark is Rising Sequence', Puffin

Doyle, Sir Arthur Conan, *The Hound of the Baskervilles*, Puffin

MISCHIEF AND MAYHEM
CHAPTER SIX

Ahlberg, Janet and Allan, *The Jolly Postman*, Heinemann

Berenstain, Stan and Jan, *The Berenstain Bears and the Missing Dinosaur Bone*, Collins

Blake, Quentin, *Mr Magnolia*, Fontana

Briggs, Raymond, *Father Christmas; Father Christmas Goes on Holiday*, Puffin

Brown, Jeff, *Flat Stanley*, Magnet
Browne, Anthony, *Bear Hunt*,
  Magnet
Burningham, John, *Mr Gumpy's
  Outing*, Puffin
Carle, Eric, *The Very Hungry
  Caterpillar*, Puffin
Cole, Babette, *Prince Cinders;
  Princess Smartypants*, Fontana
Dahl, Roald, *The BFG*, Puffin
Hergé, *The Adventures of Tintin*,
  Methuen
Hoban, Russell, and Blake,
  Quentin, *The Rain Door*,
  Gollancz
Hooper, Mary, *Lexie*, Magnet
Hutchins, Pat, *1 Hunter*, Puffin
Jones, Diana Wynne, *Eight Days of
  Luke*, Puffin
King-Smith, Dick, *The Fox Busters;
  The Sheep-Pig*, Puffin
Leeson, Robert, *The Third-Class
  Genie*, Fontana
Marray, Denis, *The Duck Street
  Gang*, Magnet
Rosen, Michael, and Baker, Alan,
  Hairy Tales and Nursery Crimes,
  Fontana
Rosen, Michael, and Blake,
  Quentin, *Don't Put Mustard in
  the Custard*, Puffin
Rowan, Peter, and Blake, Quentin,
  Ask Dr Pete, Cape
Ryan, John, *Pugwash and the Fancy
  Dress Party; Pugwash and the
  Mutiny*, Puffin
Stevenson, James, *There's Nothing
  To Do!*, Puffin
Strong, Jeremy, *The Karate Princess*,
  Black
Townsend, Sue, *The Secret Diary of
  Adrian Mole Aged 13¾*,
  Methuen
Wilson, Ron, *Stanley Bagshaw and
  the Fourteen-Foot Wheel; Stanley
  Bagshaw and the Mafeking Square
  Cheese Robbery*, Puffin
Yeoman, John, and Blake, Quentin,
  The Hermit and the Bear,
  Fontana

CLASSICS OLD AND NEW
CHAPTER SEVEN

Ardizzone, Edward, *Little Tim and
  the Brave Sea Captain*, Puffin
Barrie, J. M., *Peter Pan*, Pavilion
Bawden, Nina, *Carrie's War*, Puffin
Blume, Judy, *It's Not the End of the
  World, Blubber*, Piper
Blyton, Enid, *Five Get into Trouble;
  Five Go to Smuggler's Top*,
  Knight
Boston, Lucy, *The Children of Green
  Knowe*, Puffin
Burnett, Frances Hodgson, *The
  Secret Garden*, Puffin
Burningham, John, *Mr Gumpy's
  Outing*, Puffin
Carroll, Lewis, *Alice's Adventures in
  Wonderland*, Puffin
Dahl, Roald, *The Twits; James and
  the Giant Peach; Danny, the
  Champion of the World*, Puffin
Grahame, Kenneth, *The Wind in the
  Willows*, Puffin
Lively, Penelope, *The Ghost of
  Thomas Kempe*, Puffin
Mark, Jan, *Thunder and Lightnings*,
  Puffin
Milne, A. A., *Winnie-the-Pooh*,
  Methuen
Norton, Mary, *The Borrowers*, Puffin
Pearce, Philippa, *Tom's Midnight
  Garden*, Puffin
Potter, Beatrix, *The Tale of Jemima
  Puddle-Duck; The Tale of Mrs
  Tiggywinkle; The Tale of Peter
  Rabbit*, Warne

115

FAIRY STORIES AND FOLK STORIES

CHAPTER EIGHT

116

TEENAGE READING

CHAPTER NINE

Watson, James, *Talking in Whispers*, Fontana

Westall, Robert, *The Scarecrows*, Puffin

Zindel, Paul, *My Darling, My Hamburger*, Fontana

BOOKS AS SOCIAL COMMENT

CHAPTER TEN

Baum, Louis, and Bouma, Paddy, *Are We Nearly There?*, Magnet

Braithwaite, Althea, *When Uncle Bob Died; Going into Hospital; Starting School*, Dinosaur

Browne, Anthony, *Piggybook*, Magnet

Browne, Eileen, and Bradman, Tony, *Through My Window*, Methuen

Burnett, Frances Hodgson, *The Little Princess*, Puffin

Desai, Anita, *The Village By the Sea*, Puffin

Dhondy, Farrukh, *Come to Mecca*, Fontana

Dickinson, Mary, *Alex's Bed*, Hippo

Hamilton, Virginia, *A Little Love*, Gollancz

Howard, Ellen, *Gillyflower*, Collins

Kaye, Geraldine, *The Beautiful Take-Away Palace*, Magnet

Lloyd, Errol, *Sean's Red Bike; My Brother Sean*, Puffin

Needle, Jan, *My Mate Shofiq*, Fontana

Powling, Chris, *The Conker as Hard as a Diamond*, Puffin

Snell, Nigel, *Danny is Afraid of the Dark; Johnny Gets Some Glasses; Sally Moves House*, Hamish Hamilton

Wachter, Orale, *No More Secrets for Me*, Puffin

117

POETRY

CHAPTER ELEVEN

Causley, Charles, *Early in the Morning*, Puffin

Heaney, Seamus, Hughes, Ted (editors), *The Rattle Bag*, Faber

Ireson, Barbara, *The Young Puffin Book of Verse*, Puffin

Jackson, Holbrook, *The Complete Nonsense of Edward Lear*, Faber

McGough, Roger, *The Kingfisher Book of Comic Verse*, Kingfisher

Owen, Gareth, *Salford Road*, Fontana

Rosen, Michael, *Quick, Let's Get Out of Here!*, Puffin

Index of authors

118

119

Index of titles

121